GALLERY

GALLERY

PAULA FASSMAN

SUZANNE SEYMOUR TAVARES

New York   Oxford
OXFORD UNIVERSITY PRESS
1982

Copyright © 1982 by Oxford University Press, Inc.

Library of Congress Cataloging in Publication Data

Fassman, Paula.
  Gallery.

    1. English language—Study and teaching—
Foreign students.   I. Tavares, Suzanne Seymour.
II. Title.
PE1128.A2F29   428.2′4   82-2196
ISBN 0-19-503132-6 (pbk.)   AACR2

Notes from the English Language Teaching Department

The English Language Teaching Department of Oxford University Press, New York, is staffed by professionals with classroom experience in the fields of English as a Second Language and Bilingual Education.

It is the policy of this department to publish books and audio-visual materials that are innovative as well as professionally sound. It is in keeping with this tradition that we present *Gallery*.

We hope you enjoy our materials and find them useful for your classroom needs. Because we value the insights and experience of classroom teachers in various parts of the world, we invite you to write to us with your comments and suggestions.

The English Language Teaching Department
Oxford University Press, New York

General Manager: Marilyn Rosenthal, Ph. D.
Editors: Debbie Sistino, M.A., Margot Gramer, M.A.
Managing Editor: Vicky Bijur
Assistant Editor: Debbie Musiker
Marketing and Sales Manager: Connie Attanasio, M.S.
Assistant Marketing Manager: Gilda Cabrera, M.A.
Educational Specialists: Diana Estrada, M.A., Diane Gosser, M.A.,
    Marjorie Aiko Ono, Edwin Lamoli-Torres, M.A.
Administrative Assistant: Lenore Schaefer

Illustrations by Gerry Mooney

Printing (last digit): 9 8 7 6 5 4 3 2 1

Printed in the United States of America

ACKNOWLEDGMENTS

Our thanks to Mary Fonseca and to the staff and administration of the American Language Institute in Lisbon who helped and encouraged us on this project.

We are also grateful to Paula Korsko for her illustrations, and to Peggy Allen, Sandra Goncalves, Irene Moreira, and Susan Barduhn for their enthusiastic piloting.

A very special thanks to Jorge, Eleanor, and Kyle for their invaluable moral support.

CONTENTS

1. I Read It in the Newspaper   3
2. Panic at the Avon Hotel   11
3. Family Album   20
4. The Cardigans' Day in Court   30
5. Break-In at the Dubceks'   40
6. Ask the Experts   50
7. Spot the Dangers   59
8. Numerology   68
9. Think Fast   80
10. People and Pastimes   89
11. Darling Rosemary and Dearest Bill   100
12. The Theft of the Century   109
13. Wendy Storm's Bad Year   121
14. Clyde Tries Again   130
15. Rich Girl, Poor Boy   141
    Teacher's Notes   153

GALLERY

PRESENTATION

I READ IT IN THE NEWSPAPER

. . . he tried to rob a bank with a plastic pistol.

Robbery Attempt with Plastic Pistol

NEW YORK, Nov. 19—Clark Newton, 56, of Westbury, Connecticut, tried to rob the First National Bank of New York yesterday, using a plastic pistol. The thief went into the bank at 2 p.m., threatened customers and tellers, and told employees to hand over all the money.

Recognizing the pistol as a fake, Mike Torrijos, one of the tellers, pushed the alarm button. When the police arrived, they found Newton still inside the bank. Officers Burbadge and Carmichael handcuffed and took him to Station 48, where the thief is now awaiting trial. When asked why he had attempted such a foolish plan, Newton replied, "I needed the money to buy a real gun."

Blind Surgeon Wins Award

STOCKHOLM, Oct. 3—Dr. Paul Brent of the Spokes Institute won the International Surgeon's Award in Stockholm last night. Dr. Brent was born in Grand Rapids, Michigan, in 1927, and graduated from the University of Toronto Medical School in 1952.

Totally blind since birth, Dr. Brent studied medical texts in braille and had to learn surgical techniques solely through his sense of touch. Dr. Ames Aubrey, President of the New York College of Medicine where Brent taught from 1956 to 1966, said of his colleague, "Despite all his problems, he became the best surgeon at the College and earned the love and respect of everyone who worked with him."

1. Read the article.
2. Retell the story as if you were a witness to the robbery. You may be a bank teller, customer, or man-on-the-street.
3. You are a reporter. Interview Officers Burbadge and Carmichael using the following question words: *How old, What time, Who, What, Where, When, Why, How.*

1. Read the article.
2. Imagine you are Dr. Brent and that you are recounting the events in the newspaper article in the first person.
3. You are a reporter. Interview Dr. Aubrey using the following question words: *Where, When, How long, How, What.*

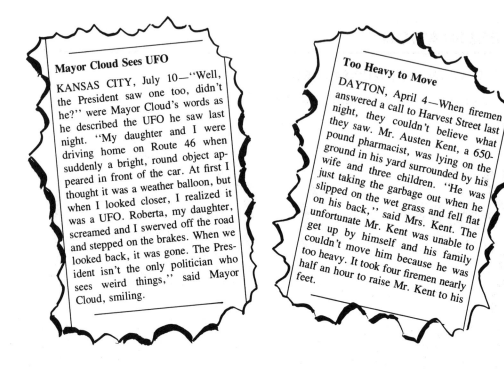

Mayor Cloud Sees UFO

KANSAS CITY, July 10—"Well, the President saw one too, didn't he?" were Mayor Cloud's words as he described the UFO he saw last night. "My daughter and I were driving home on Route 46 when suddenly a bright, round object appeared in front of the car. At first I thought it was a weather balloon, but when I looked closer, I realized it was a UFO. Roberta, my daughter, screamed and I swerved off the road and stepped on the brakes. When we looked back, it was gone. The President isn't the only politician who sees weird things," said Mayor Cloud, smiling.

Too Heavy to Move

DAYTON, April 4—When firemen answered a call to Harvest Street last night, they couldn't believe what they saw. Mr. Austen Kent, a 650-pound pharmacist, was lying on the ground in his yard surrounded by his wife and three children. "He was just taking the garbage out when he slipped on the wet grass and fell flat on his back," said Mrs. Kent. The unfortunate Mr. Kent was unable to get up by himself and his family couldn't move him because he was too heavy. It took four firemen nearly half an hour to raise Mr. Kent to his feet.

1. Read the article.
2. Retell the story pretending you are the Mayor's daughter, Roberta.
3. You are a reporter. Interview Mayor Cloud using the following question words: *Who, When, Where, What.*

1. Read the article.
2. Retell the story pretending you are Austen Kent.
3. You are a reporter. Interview Mrs. Kent using the following question words: *When, How much, What, Why, How long.*

EXPANSION

Read the following story or listen while your teacher reads it aloud.

Mystery Story

He was calm, very calm. He got up at the usual time that morning, shaved, took a shower, and got dressed. After glancing at the headlines in the morning paper, he drank a cup of coffee, but he couldn't force himself to eat. Even though it was still very early, he put on his hat and coat and left the house.

"I want to make a change in my will," he said calmly, "a change that will be effective immediately."

He was still quite calm as he left the lawyer's office and walked slowly toward the park. It was a cloudy, humid day. He began to think about his decision. He also thought about his wife and all the long, unhappy years they had spent together.

It was after six when he arrived home. He took off his hat and coat, poured himself a drink, sat down on the sofa, and waited.

"You're home," said his wife as she opened the door. "How was your day?"

"Oh, the same as usual," he replied as he kissed her. Then she went into the kitchen to prepare dinner.

He walked to his desk, opened a drawer, and took out a gun. Then the neighbors heard a shot.

1. Reconstruct the story by asking questions about what "he" did that day. Use the following question words: *How, What, When, What kind.*

Examples: How did he feel that morning?
He felt . . .

What did he do after he got up?
After he got up, he . . .

2. What do you think actually happened? Who died—the man or his wife? Give reasons for your decision.

GRAMMAR SUMMARY

THE SIMPLE PAST TENSE

	AFFIRMATIVE	INTERROGATIVE	NEGATIVE
Regular Verbs	They wait*ed* for the bus for 20 minutes. (base form + *-ed*)	How long *did* they *wait* for the bus? (*did* + base form)	They *didn't wait* very long. (*did* + *not* + base form)
Irregular Verbs	She *took* a sedative before going to bed. He *went* to the movies. They *heard* a shot. (no rule)	How many sedatives *did* she *take?* Where *did* he *go?* What *did* they *hear?* (*did* + base form)	She *didn't take* very many. He *didn't go* to school. They *didn't hear* a scream. (*did* + *not* + base form)

Notes

i. When the question word (*Who, What,* etc.) is the subject of the question, do not use the auxiliary *did.*

Examples: What happened? Who shot her? Who gave you those flowers? How many people came?

ii. Pronunciation of regular verbs:

/t/ walked, looked, laughed, talked, washed, helped, smoked, cooked, asked, stopped, danced, reached, dropped, worked, picked.

/d/ closed, phoned, married, carried, stayed, arrived, died, studied, opened, used, played, borrowed, traveled.

/ɪd/ started, pointed, sounded, counted, waited, repeated, corrected, wanted, ended, expected, treated, visited.

iii. Spelling:
Many verbs ending in *y* drop the *y* and replace it with *i* before the *-ed* is added.

Examples: dry/dried   carry/carried   study/studied   marry/married

If the stress in a polysyllabic word is on the first syllable, the final consonant is not doubled before *-ed.*

Examples: kidnap/kidnaped   travel/traveled

If the stress occurs on the second syllable, the final consonant is doubled.

Example: regret/regretted

INTENSIVE PRACTICE

I. Complete the following sentences using the example below as a model.

Example: (paint) I _____ the house, but I _____ the garage.
I *painted* the house, but I *didn't paint* the garage.

1. (call)   She _____ the fire department, but she _____ an ambulance.
2. (visit) I _____ my Aunt Martha, but I _____ my Uncle Harry.
3. (enjoy) We _____ the book, but we _____ the film.
4. (wash)   He _____ his face, but he _____ his hands.
5. (lock)   I _____ the front door, but I _____ the back door.

II. Complete the following sentences using the example below as a model.

Example: (take)   She ——————— a vitamin pill, but she ——————— a sedative.
She *took* a vitamin pill, but she *didn't take* a sedative.

1. (buy)   I ——————— the bread, but I ——————— the rice.
2. (read)   She ——————— the first book, but she ——————— the second one.
3. (bring)   He ——————— the documents, but he ——————— the money.
4. (write)   I ——————— to my brother, but I ——————— to my sister.
5. (win)   They ——————— their first game, but they ——————— their second.
6. (wear)   He ——————— a coat, but he ——————— a sweater.
7. (lend)   I ——————— him my umbrella, but I ——————— him my car.
8. (understand)   She ——————— the first exercise, but she ——————— the second one.
9. (choose)   He ——————— a beautiful dress for his wife, but he ——————— the right color.
10. (lose)   He ——————— the first race, but he ——————— the second one.

III. Using the example below as a model, complete the following:

Example: A: I never catch the bus to work.
B: Come on! *You caught the bus to work yesterday.*

1. A: I never drink wine for lunch.
   B: Come on! ————————————————————————.
2. A: I never take more than two coffee breaks.
   B: Come on! ————————————————————————.
3. A: I never give money to that man.
   B: Come on! ————————————————————————.
4. A: I never keep the heat on at night.
   B: Come on! ————————————————————————.
5. A: My dog never bites the mailman.
   B: Come on! ————————————————————————.

IV. Create dialogues using the following cues and an appropriate verb.

Example: English or French lessons
A: Did you take English or French lessons?
B: I took French lessons.
A: Why didn't you take English lessons?
B: Because English is too hard.

1. the blue coat or the green one
2. a birthday card or a telegram
3. the subway or the bus

4. a concert or the movies
5. a Porsche or a Ferrari
6. a steak or fried fish
7. a Coke or a cup of coffee
8. alone or in a chorus
9. a novel or a poem
10. on TWA or Iberia

V. Create short dialogues beginning:
A: Guess what my brother did the other day?
B: I don't know. What did he do?

Example: a very expensive vase
A: Guess what my brother did the other day?
B: I don't know. What did he do?
A: He broke a very expensive vase.

1. his wife's birthday
2. a very important examination
3. the train to Paris
4. a lot of money at the casino
5. ten aspirins

WRITING AND HOMEWORK

I. Complete the following story by filling in the blanks with an appropriate verb in the past tense.

Marvin _____ the bus, _____ down the block, and absent-mindedly _____ on the door of one of the several cream-colored suburban houses. "Nobody's home," he thought to himself. He _____ to open the door with his key, but it _____ (negative) and so he _____ the knob and _____ inside.
   "Anne, where are you?" he _____ to his wife. Nobody _____ so he _____ down, _____ up the newspaper, and _____ it from beginning to end. When he _____ reading the newspaper, he _____ up, _____ himself a drink and _____ on the TV. "Where can she be?" he _____, half worried, half puzzled. "Well, I suppose she's at her mother's again."
   He _____ asleep in the chair and slowly the street _____ dark and the street lights _____ on outside. He _____ soundly until he _____ someone shaking him. "Mr. Rafferty, what are you doing here?" It _____ his neighbor, Mrs. Coogan. "Your wife _____ to the police an hour ago to report you missing."
   "You mean I _____ the wrong house?" he _____ incredulously. "I _____ all suburban houses looked alike inside and out, but this is ridiculous!"

II. This is a page from the diary of Hans Schmidt, the Foreign Minister from Lebensraum. Write a report on what he did last Friday. You do not need to mention the precise time of all his activities.

<u>Friday, March 4</u>

10:00 Arrive Washington, D.C.
10:45 Check in—Hotel Columbia
11:15 Conference—Middle East crisis
12:00 Meeting—President
 1:00 Lunch—British Ambassador
 2:00 Call Dr. Rother—checkup
 3:00 Phone Judith
 4:00 Sedative
 5:00 Harris and Thompson's—new suit
 6:00 Cocktails—Thai Ambassador
 7:00 Dinner—Judith
 8:00 Bongo Club
 9:00 Sedative

III. Read the following newspaper article:

One evening, Mrs. Philip Jennings began complaining to her husband about some severe back pains that she had been having all day. Mr. Jennings, who had recently read an article about the benefits of hypnotism, decided to try and help his wife. That evening he hypnotized her, and when he asked if she felt any better, she answered him in a strange language. Mr. Jennings ran and got a tape recorder and began to tape what she was saying. Over a period of two weeks, in flawless Welsh, Mrs. Jennings described her past life as a schoolgirl in Cardiff in the late 19th century.

Write a similar story about Jack Wilkins. He suffered from headaches, and when his wife tried to hypnotize him she made an astonishing discovery. Use your own ideas.

DISCUSSION

I. Choose one of the following to tell in class. You may want to spend a few minutes making notes first.

1. a joke
2. an embarrassing experience
3. the most frightening experience of your life
4. a legend or fairy tale
5. an annoying experience

II. Find an interesting newspaper article, either in English or in any other language, and read it at home. Be prepared to tell the class in English about what you have read.

BITS AND PIECES

Even though

I. Combine the following sentences using *even though*.

Example: It was still quite early. He put on his hat and coat and left the house.

Even though it was still quite early, he put on his hat and coat and left the house.

1. It was cold. He wasn't wearing a coat.
2. He hadn't eaten all day. He refused to have dinner with us.
3. He was sick. He went to school.
4. She was on a diet. She said she wanted more cake.
5. He earns a lot of money. He's always borrowing from his friends.

II. Combine the following sentences using *even though* and *managed to*.

Example: He was seriously wounded. He saved his dog.

Even though he was seriously wounded, he managed to save his dog.

1. The test was difficult. He passed it.
2. They lost their best player. They won the game.
3. They weren't good swimmers. They swam to shore.
4. They were late. They caught the train in time.
5. The man had been shot four times. The doctors saved his life.

III. Harry Houdini was the stage name of one of America's greatest escape artists. He was known around the world as the man who could escape from anything. His feats were truly extraordinary. On several occasions they locked him in chains, tied him with ropes, put him in prison, threw him tied up into a tank of water, and put him in a straitjacket, but he got out every time—usually in a few minutes.

On other occasions he was tied up and suspended by ropes from a small plane, or thrown into the ocean in chains without an air supply, but he always got to safety. There have been many escape artists since Houdini, but none have been able to repeat his fabulous feats.

Make at least five sentences about Houdini from the above story, using *even though* and *managed to*.

Example: Even though they locked him in chains, he managed to open them and escape.

PRESENTATION

PANIC AT THE AVON HOTEL

. . . I was reading a newspaper when the ceiling fell in.

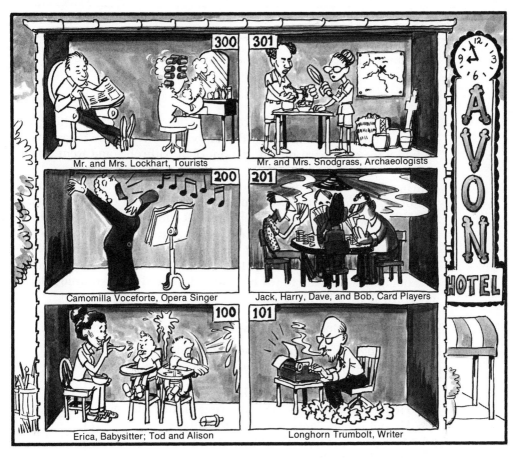

Mr. and Mrs. Lockhart, Tourists

Mr. and Mrs. Snodgrass, Archaeologists

Camomilla Voceforte, Opera Singer

Jack, Harry, Dave, and Bob, Card Players

Erica, Babysitter; Tod and Alison

Longhorn Trumbolt, Writer

I. This is a cross section of the Avon Hotel at 8:55 p.m. At 8:56 a bomb went off causing great damage but no loss of life. Using the following cues, tell what the guests were doing at the time.

Example: Mr. Lockhart was reading a newspaper when the bomb exploded.

bomb/explode	windows/break *or* shatter
walls/crumble	fire/start
building/shake	ceiling/fall in
	lights/go off

II. Now take the parts of the people involved in the disaster. Refer to the pictures, but use your own ideas when completing the dialogue.

Example: STUDENT 1 (*as reporter*): What were you doing when the walls crumbled, Mr. Lockhart?
STUDENT 2 (*as Lockhart*): I was sitting and reading a newspaper.

STUDENT 1: And what did you do then?
STUDENT 2: I ran out of my room as fast as I could.

EXPANSION

Read the following short story or listen as your teacher reads it aloud.

Bad Luck

I was taking a shower the other day when the doorbell rang. There was water on the bathroom floor and I slipped and fell while I was trying to find a towel. I dried myself off, put on a bathrobe, and went downstairs.

When I opened the door, no one was there. While I was standing at the door, scratching my head and wondering who it could have been, my little dog ran out. I ran after him, but the door closed behind me and I didn't have my keys. I was locked out, wearing only my bathrobe.

A window on the second floor was open, so I found a ladder. While I was climbing the ladder, a policeman saw me and asked me what I was doing. I was trying to tell him when I noticed water running down my front steps. I had forgotten to turn off the water!

Correct the following statements without referring to the text.

Example: He was reading the newspaper when the doorbell rang.
That's not right. He was taking a shower when the doorbell rang.

1. There was perfume on the bathroom floor.
2. He hit his head while he was trying to find a towel.
3. He put on his pants and went upstairs.
4. A salesman was at the door.
5. His wife ran out of the house.
6. The door stayed open.
7. He had his keys with him.
8. All the windows were closed.
9. A neighbor saw him while he was climbing down the ladder.
10. He noticed smoke coming out from under the door.

GRAMMAR SUMMARY

THE PAST CONTINUOUS

AFFIRMATIVE		INTERROGATIVE		
I was You were He/She was We were They were	listening to the radio last night.	What	were you was he/she were we were they	doing when the accident happened?
NEGATIVE				
I wasn't You weren't He/She wasn't We weren't They weren't	talking on the phone for three hours last night.			

    I. The past continuous is used to indicate an extended or continued action in the past.

   II. It is often used with *while* or *when* and interrupted by a short past action.

     A. *While* always introduces the extended action.

Example: While he was taking a bath, the phone rang.

     B. *When* can introduce either the interrupting action or the extended action.

Examples: He was taking a bath when the phone rang.
            When he was taking a bath, the phone rang.

   III. Two simultaneous extended past actions may also be used together.

Example: While I was washing the dishes, they were doing their homework.

Notes: Spelling

Most verbs ending in *e* drop the *e* before *-ing* is added.

Examples: *taking, having, typing, giving, coming, phoning, closing, arriving, making, dancing, using, biting.*

Many verbs have a vowel before the final consonant. This consonant is usually doubled before *-ing* is added.

Examples: *running, stopping, digging, knitting, begging.*

If the stress in a polysyllabic verb is on the first syllable, the final consonant is not doubled before *-ing*, e.g. *quarreling, kidnaping, traveling.* If the stress occurs on the second syllable, the final consonant is doubled, e.g. *forgetting, regretting.*

INTENSIVE PRACTICE

I. Make sentences using the following cues. Make a *while* and a *when* sentence for *each* cue.

Example: I/out the window   see an accident

While I was looking out the window, I saw an accident.

and

I was looking out the window when I saw an accident.

1. I/a shower	hear the doorbell ring
2. he/dinner	burn himself
3. I/television	hear a strange noise outside
4. Jack/home from work	run out of gas
5. she/onions	cut herself
6. he/his homework	the lights go out
7. she/the attic	find a rare old book
8. they/breakfast	the milkman arrive
9. she/some candy	break her tooth
10. we/the bus	begin to rain

II. Make two questions from the following sets of cues:

Example: come to school   feel ill

Why didn't you come to school? Were you feeling ill?

1. come on time	work late
2. hear the phone ring	practice the piano
3. the driver see the victim	wear dark clothes
4. stop in time	drive too fast
5. hear what he said	speak too softly

III. Create dialogues using the cues provided. Make sure to use correct intonation.

Example: Bernard   theater

A: I saw Bernard at the theater last night.
B: No kidding! What was he doing there?
A: What do you think he was doing? He was watching a play, of course.

1. Margaret	airport
2. Jack	bar
3. Frank and Mary	library
4. Harvey	bookstore
5. Rita	dentist
6. Carol	Chez Lui Restaurant
7. Jean and Jane	post office
8. Mike	barber's
9. Mr. Lewis	Yankee Stadium
10. Mr. and Mrs. Hopper	church

IV. Complete the following questions and answers. Numbers 1–6 are affirmative.

Example: Why   Ted and Lou _____ their old car
               too much gasoline

Why did Ted and Lou sell their old car?
Because it was using too much gasoline.

Numbers 7–10 are negative.

Example: Why   boss _____ the salesman a better job?
               enough vacuum cleaners.

Why didn't the boss give the salesman a better job?
Because he wasn't selling enough vacuum cleaners.

1. Why   the policeman _____ Mr. Smith a traffic ticket?
   with his headlights off
2. Why   the librarian _____ the boys?
   too much noise
3. Why   Jane _____ angry with her boyfriend?
   with other girls
4. Why   Doris _____ her little girl?
   with matches
5. Why   Peter Carson _____ his wife?
   another man
6. Why   the manager _____ Tom out of the theater?
   in the no-smoking section
7. Why   the boss _____ him a raise?   (negative)
   his job properly
8. Why   Gloria _____ the stop sign?   (negative)
   her glasses
9. Why   the doorman _____ Tom into the casino?   (negative)
   a jacket and a tie
10. Why   Bill _____ the question?   (negative)
    attention to the teacher

V. Complete the following dialogues using the example as a model.

Example: A: What _____ doing _____ doorbell (ring)?
              B: I _____ the newspaper.
              A: the door right away?
              B: No . . . a few minutes later.

              A: What were you doing when the doorbell rang?
              B: I was reading the newspaper.
              A: Did you answer the door right away?
              B: No, I answered it a few minutes later.

1. A: What _____ doing _____ burglars (break) in?
   B: I _____ my homework.
   A: the police right away?
   B: No . . . the morning after.

2. A: What _____ doing _____ house (catch) fire?
   B: I _____ dinner.
   A: out of the house right away?
   B: No . . . after collecting my things.
3. A: What _____ doing _____ (break) your leg?
   B: I _____ a tree.
   A: hospital right away?
   B: No . . . after the ambulance arrived.
4. A: What _____ doing _____ tornado (hit)?
   B: I _____ the dishes.
   A: the house right away?
   B: No . . . after it was over.
5. A: What _____ doing _____ earthquake (strike)?
   B: I _____ ready for bed.
   A: the children's room right away?
   B: No . . . when it stopped.

VI. Repeat the first sentence and then construct a second, using the cue provided. Make sure to stress the italicized words.

Example: I wasn't copying *Lisa's* paper. (*Jane's*)

I wasn't copying *Lisa's* paper. I was copying *Jane's*.

1. I wasn't reading *father's* mail.	(*yours*)
2. *I* wasn't making all that noise.	(*Peter*)
3. We weren't speaking *Portuguese* to him.	(*English*)
4. He wasn't trying to *steal* the car.	(*unlock*)
5. *Our* dog wasn't howling all night.	(*theirs*)
6. We weren't swimming at the *pool*.	(*beach*)
7. I wasn't using *your* pen.	(*Jack's*)
8. I wasn't reading a *newspaper*.	(*magazine*)
9. He wasn't *buying* the watch.	(*selling*)
10. It wasn't *in* the refrigerator.	(*on*)

WRITING AND HOMEWORK

I. Linda Mitchell and her husband George had a "come as you are" party last night. Linda phoned all the guests at eight o'clock and said, "We're having a party! Come as soon as you can, and COME AS YOU ARE!"
The guests arrived like this:

1. Mary was wearing an apron.
2. Jim was wearing pajamas.
3. Larry had only one of his shoes on.
4. John and Rita came with coffee cups in their hands.
5. Frank had shaving cream all over his face.
6. Barbara's hair was wet.

7. Fred came with a towel wrapped around him.
8. Ron had a thermometer in his mouth.
9. Peter had a stamp stuck to his tongue.
10. Murray had a spoon in his mouth.

What do you think the guests were doing when Linda phoned to invite them to the party?

II. Extend the following conversation by supplying the missing words.

MR. POLLOCK: I was _____ in the back yard _____ the newspaper when suddenly the sky _____ dark. _____ really frightening!

REPORTER: What _____ think _____ happening?

MRS. POLLOCK: We _____ that a cyclone _____ hit.

MR. GOLDBERG: Yes. We _____ too. My wife _____ the piano and the kids _____ in the yard when the sky _____ black and—

MRS. GOLDBERG: First we _____ a loud noise, remember, dear? Like the roar of a jet plane.

REPORTER: What _____ you do?

MRS. GOLDBERG: I _____ outside and _____ the kids to get into the house.

REPORTER: What _____ you doing, Mrs. Davis?

MRS. DAVIS: I _____ dinner, _____ the potatoes to be precise, when Jack _____ me if I had _____ a loud noise.

MR. DAVIS: Yeah! The kids and I _____ a model plane. We all stopped and _____ outside.

REPORTER: And then what _____ see?

MR. DAVIS: The Pollocks and the Goldbergs were outside too. We _____ all _____ up at the sky when the noise _____ louder.

MRS. POLLOCK: And then we _____ it! _____ bigger than a floating ship and _____ rotating and flashing on and off.

REPORTER: _____ moving back and forth?

MR. POLLOCK: No, _____ . It _____ just hovering in the air over our houses.

REPORTER: _____ afraid, huh?

MR. GOLDBERG: Well, it's not every day you see a UFO, and I personally _____ to wait around to be captured by little green men!

III. Choose one of the following incidents and write an interview between a reporter and several people who were there. You may wish to refer to Exercise II for ideas. Be sure to use the question words: *Who, What, When, Where, How* and *Why* as you conduct your interview.

—a robbery
—a car accident
—a plane crash

DISCUSSION

I. Read and discuss the following statements made by people who have experienced earthquakes:

"I thought I would panic in a disaster, but when the earthquake struck, my husband broke down and I managed to stay calm. My 'reason' seemed to take over, and I found that I was able to calm other people down."

Rosemary Benvenuto, Housewife.

"When it came, I started to pray, yes, pray. I thought I didn't believe in God, but when I thought that I was going to die, I actually started to pray."

Clifford Saxon, Engineer.

"The ground started to shake, and there I was, on the street next to the tallest building in the city. I ran and ran, and as I did, I thought, 'Why do they build such tall structures in earthquake zones?' "

T. Suzuki, Mechanic.

"And then I noticed what was so strange. All the birds had left the city. They seemed to know the earthquake was coming, and they left. Animals have a sixth sense about these things."

Marianne Morris (San Francisco earthquake)

". . . and some of us think that underground nuclear testing has a great effect on seismic activity."

Roberta Ellis, Geologist.

II. Discuss the following:

1. Most people have a morbid fascination with accidents or disasters. Recently in New York City, a crowd gathered outside an office building where a man on a ledge on the 19th floor was threatening to commit suicide. The crowd started shouting, "Jump! Jump!" as if it wanted to be entertained.
2. It is said that violence in films and TV shows causes people to commit acts of violence. What is your opinion?

BITS AND PIECES

. . . would you like me to . . . ?   . . . should I . . . ?

    I. Complete the following by using *would you like me to* and *should I* after the question words.

Example: Where/these books?

Where would you like me to put these books?   *and*

Where should I put these books?

1. What time _____ phone you?

2. How much wine _____ bring?

3. Where _____ meet you?

4. How much food _____ buy?

5. How many people _____ invite?

6. When _____ pick you up?

7. What _____ do?

8. Where _____ hang your coat?

9. What sweater _____ wear?

10. How many letters _____ type?

    II. Philip's Aunt Agatha has just arrived to pay him a visit. She is a very difficult old lady to get along with. She complains constantly and expects everyone to jump when she gives orders. Philip, however, is always *very* nice to her. He goes out of his way to please her. Maybe it's because she's a millionaire!

AUNT AGATHA: It's freezing in this house! How can you stand to live in this . . . this refrigerator?

PHILIP: Would you like me to | get you a sweater?
       Should I | turn up the heat?
                   | close the window?

Continue their conversation as Aunt Agatha complains that:

—she doesn't feel well

—she's hungry

—she's thirsty

—she isn't comfortable

—she doesn't like a picture that is on the living room wall

Use *would you like me to* and *should I* for Philip's part of the conversation as he desperately tries to please her.

PRESENTATION

FAMILY ALBUM

I remember Cousin Sarah. She used to read her horoscope all the time.

SUPERSTITIOUS COUSIN SARAH
—a rabbit's foot
—knock on wood
—her horoscope

RICH UNCLE HENRY
—expensive suits
—expensive cigars
—trips to the Orient

KIND AUNT BERTHA
—candy
—her money to charity
—homeless dogs

COUSIN SARAH UNCLE FRED
UNCLE HENRY COUSIN PHIL
AUNT BERTHA COUSIN MARTIN

ABSENT-MINDED UNCLE FRED
—his overcoat behind
—on the wrong bus
—to comb his hair

COUSIN PHIL, THE GAMBLER
—his salary
—money from his friends
—Sunday afternoons at the racetrack

COUSIN MARTIN THE GLUTTON
—for second helpings
—on low-calorie diets
—ice-cream and cake between meals

John, Mary, Pamela, and Michael are looking through an old family album and talking about their relatives.

I. Practice the model dialogue, taking the parts of John, Mary, Michael, and Pamela.

JOHN: Look at this picture of superstitious Cousin Sarah! Remember her?
MARY: How could I ever forget! She would always have a rabbit's foot with her.
PAMELA: Yes, and she was always knocking on wood, too.
MICHAEL: And I remember that she used to read her horoscope all the time.

II. Using the model dialogue as a reference, make similar conversations with the cues provided.

EXPANSION

Read and discuss the following text.

His Favorite Cousin

Horace was very proud of his cousin, Mike Aspen, Hollywood's brightest young star. Whenever his cousin appeared on the screen, Horace would say, "Isn't he wonderful? He's my cousin, you know."

What was worse, Horace was always cutting pictures of his cousin out of movie magazines and putting them on the kitchen wall. His wife would say, "We used to have a nice clean wall. Now all I can see is Mike, Mike, Mike!" Then she would walk angrily out of the kitchen and slam the door behind her.

When Mike's face used to appear on posters or billboards, Horace would proudly brag about his cousin's successful career. "He used to go to Midville High School, you know. We would always play in the school yard together, and we were always getting into trouble together. I remember how he was always stealing apples from the corner grocery store. He used to be like a brother to me. We were always missing classes together. What a great guy, a truly great guy. He was my favorite cousin."

One day, though, everyone woke up to find the daily newspapers covered with the headlines, MIKE ASPEN INVOLVED IN GANGLAND KILLING. Reporters went to Horace's house to interview him. "Did you and Mike Aspen really use to be like brothers? Is it true you were both getting into trouble all the time? What kind of trouble? Did you really play in the school yard together?"

"Mike Aspen . . . Mike Aspen . . . ," he said in a puzzled voice. "Oh yes! The actor." Horace shook his head, "No relation to me. Never met the guy."

Using the cues on the right, make *Who* questions. Then give a short answer to each question. You will find *would, was always,* or *used to* in parentheses after each cue. Use these to form the questions.

Example 1   out of the kitchen   *(would always)*
A: Who would always walk out of the kitchen?
B: Horace's wife would.

Example 2   together as children   *(used to)*
A: Who used to play together as children?
B: Horace and Mike did.

   1. the kitchen door   *(would always)*
   2. about his cousin's career   *(would always)*
   3. to Midville High School   *(used to)*
   4. on the screen   *(used to)*
   5. in the school yard   *(used to)*
   6. pictures of Mike out of movie magazines   *(was always)*

    7. into trouble   *(was always)*
    8. apples from the corner grocery store   *(was always)*
    9. pictures of Mike on the wall   *(was always)*
  10. classes together   *(was always)*

GRAMMAR SUMMARY

HABIT IN THE PAST

used to do, would do, was always doing

  I. Used to
    Used + the infinitive indicates a past routine, a discontinued past habit, or a prolonged state in the past.
    A. A past routine:

Example: When I worked on that farm in Connecticut, *I used to get up* at five in the morning, and *I used to eat* an enormous breakfast before going out to work.

    B. A discontinued past habit:

Example: *I used to smoke* a lot, but I don't any more.

                I used to visit my parents every weekend, but now I see them once every six months.

    C. A prolonged state in the past:

Example: *He used to have* a beard, but he shaved it off.

                She used to be a good tennis player when she was young.

Notes

  i. Instead of the negative form, *She didn't use to study very hard,* a negation is often made with *never:*

Example: She *never used to* study very hard.

  ii. The negative-interrogative form is frequently employed as a confirmation question:

Example: *Didn't she use to* live across the street from you?

  iii. Many people, even native speakers, often mistakenly write *used to* with a *d* even in the negative and interrogative forms. The *d* is written only in the affirmative.

Examples: *I used to* see him every day. (affirmative)

               Didn't you use to go to school in Pittsburgh? (negative-interrogative)

II. Would (do)

Would + the base form of the verb indicates a past routine or a habit in the past.

A. It can be used interchangeably with *used to* to indicate a past routine or habit, and is often accompanied by *usually* or *always*. The contracted form is commonly used.

Example: When I worked on that farm in Connecticut, *I would get up* at five o'clock in the morning and *I'd eat* an enormous breakfast before going out to work. At night *I'd be* so tired that I could hardly stay awake past nine.

B. When a past routine is being narrated, *would* and *used to* are often used in the same narrative in order to avoid the constant repetition of either.

Example: *We used to spend* hours working on that old car. Harry would come over to my house right after school, and *we'd start working*. He used to tell his parents that we were studying together, but *we'd never even open* our school books.

Notes

i. The interrogative form is rarely used, and the negative is usually formed by adding *never*, e.g. *I would never disobey* my father when I was a child.

ii. The *would* form can only be used to indicate a past routine or a habit in the past. It is not usually employed, however, if the habit is emphasized as being discontinued, and it cannot be used to indicate a prolonged state in the past.

Examples: He *would work* on his car every evening.   (past habit)

He *used to work* on his car every evening, but now he goes to the movies.   (past habit discontinued)

He *used to be* a mechanic, but he isn't any more.   (prolonged state in the past, discontinued)

III. Was/Were always (. . . ing)

A. The past continuous with *always* is also commonly used to indicate a past routine or a habit in the past, e.g.

Example: He *was always following* me around when we were kids.

B. The *was/were always* (. . . *ing*) form is often used with a frequently repeated past action when the speaker is criticizing this action or expressing his annoyance or disapproval, e.g.

Examples: She *was always borrowing* money from me when we were in school.
They *were always getting* into trouble.

Notes

i. This form is more commonly used in the affirmative than in the interrogative or negative.

ii. Following the same rule as *would (do)* in II (ii), this form cannot be used to indicate a prolonged state in the past, and is not commonly employed when a habit is emphasized as being discontinued. It is used only in past routines or to indicate habit in the past.

INTENSIVE PRACTICE

I. Make three sentences from each of the following. Employ *used to, would always,* and *was always.*

Examples: She _____ silly questions when she was in high school.

She used to ask silly questions when she was in high school.

She would always ask silly questions when she was in high school.

She was always asking silly questions when she was in high school.

1. Heather _____ other people's papers during exams.
2. Carla _____ tricks on her friends when she was a child.
3. Mark and Carl _____ bad jokes at parties.
4. They _____ mistakes when they were in college.
5. He _____ me flowers when we were first married.
6. She _____ lies when she was a child.
7. They _____ into trouble when they were kids.
8. She _____ Beatles records when she lived in New York.
9. They _____ backaches when they had that hard bed.
10. She _____ the wrong bus when she was in New York.
11. He _____ his sister's records when they were teenagers.
12. They _____ cocktail parties when they lived in Chicago.

II. Complete the following with *used to* and the negative-interrogative.

Examples: you _____ on Queen Street?

Didn't you use to live on Queen Street?

1. she _____ school in Boston?
2. your brother _____ at the British Institute?
3. she _____ your best friend?
4. your sister _____ in an apartment in Chicago?
5. your parents _____ their vacations in Florida?
6. that man _____ football for the Toronto Tigers?
7. they _____ a big house in the country?
8. you _____ a red sports car?

III. Use *was always* and *would always* in the following school situations.

Example: Carl   miss classes

I remember Carl. He was always missing classes.

I remember Carl. He would always miss classes.

1. Bob   fall asleep in French class
2. that girl   have trouble with math
3. John   fight in class
4. those boys   irritate the teachers
5. them   throw food in the cafeteria
6. him   forget to do his homework
7. that boy   give the right answer
8. her   ask stupid questions
9. him   daydream in English class
10. those girls come late to class

IV. Make two sentences from the cues provided. Employ only *used to* and
pay attention to the verb changes.

Examples: He was a doctor, but ＿＿＿＿＿＿. Now ＿＿＿＿＿a college profes-
sor.
He used to be a doctor, but he isn't any more.
Now he's a college professor.
They drank wine with their meals but ＿＿＿＿＿＿. Now
＿＿＿＿＿＿beer.
They used to drink wine with their meals, but they don't any more.
Now they drink beer.

1. They worked for the phone company, but ＿＿＿＿＿＿. Now
＿＿＿＿＿＿the electric company.
2. They liked chocolate ice cream, but ＿＿＿＿＿＿. Now
＿＿＿＿＿＿strawberry ice cream.
3. Jack and Sandra were Dr. Hammer's patients, but ＿＿＿＿＿＿.
Now ＿＿＿＿＿＿Dr. Gold's.
4. They thought that French was the easiest language to learn, but
＿＿＿＿＿＿. Now ＿＿＿＿＿＿English.
5. He believed in Plato's philosophy, but ＿＿＿＿＿＿. Now
＿＿＿＿＿＿Sartre's.
6. She was the best student, but ＿＿＿＿＿＿. Now ＿＿＿＿＿＿the
worst.
7. They considered Galileo to be a fool, but ＿＿＿＿＿＿. Now
＿＿＿＿＿＿a genius.
8. He had a Rolls Royce, but ＿＿＿＿＿＿. Now ＿＿＿＿＿＿a
Porsche.
9. They lived in Buenos Aires, but ＿＿＿＿＿＿. Now
＿＿＿＿＿＿Montevideo.
10. They were always on time, but ＿＿＿＿＿＿. Now
＿＿＿＿＿＿late.
11. There was a movie theatre on Oak Street, but ＿＿＿＿＿＿, Now
＿＿＿＿＿＿a coffee shop.
12. He was the captain of the football team, but ＿＿＿＿＿＿. Now
＿＿＿＿＿＿the coach.
13. People believed the world was flat, but ＿＿＿＿＿＿. Now
＿＿＿＿＿＿round.

14. There were two lamps in the living room, but ——————. Now ——————only one.
15. She got up early every day, but ——————. Now ——————late.

V. The Carter family is remembering rich Uncle Kevin. Using the following cues, make sentences about Uncle Kevin with *would always*. Preface each sentence with one of the exclamations on the right. Choose the exclamation that suits the cue best.

Examples: bed with his hat on
What a weird guy! He would always go to bed with his hat on.

expensive Turkish cigarettes
He really knew how to live! He would always smoke expensive Turkish cigarettes.

lots of presents for Christmas
What a great guy! He would always bring us lots of presents for Christmas.

Exclamations

1. bed with his shoes on
2. caviar for lunch
3. us expensive presents for Christmas
4. the whole afternoon in museums
5. us stories about his trips around the world
6. collect old bottle tops
7. the summer on his own private island
8. brandy with his coffee
9. to our house in a big limousine
10. pictures of us in his wallet
11. expensive Italian suits
12. donate $5,000 to charity every year

What a weird guy!
He really knew how to live!
What a great guy

WRITING AND HOMEWORK

I. Complete the following.

Used to

1. When we lived on the farm, we ——————— at six o'clock every morning.
2. He ——————— a blue sports car, but he sold it.
3. Mary ——————— at the University of Wisconsin, but she doesn't any more.
4. Harry ——————— a fantastic swimmer, but he isn't any more.
5. When Jack and I were kids, we ——————— our homework together.

Was/were always or would always

1. Aunt Harriet ——————— jokes whenever she went to a party.
2. They ——————— into trouble when they were teenagers.
3. My sister ——————— late for her classes when she was a student.
4. She ——————— expensive clothes when she worked for Acme Inc.
5. They ——————— champagne for breakfast when they were rich.

II. There are several verbs missing from the following story. Expand the story by using *used to, would,* or *was/were always* with an appropriate verb. You will also have to use the past tense in certain places. Use the small letters and the key at the end of the story to help you complete the text.

My husband and I (a) a parrot when we lived in Chicago. My husband (b) to teach it how to talk. He (c) for hours in front of its cage, but the parrot never (d) anything.

The month after we bought it, I (d) to hear squawking noises at night in our bedroom. Every night just after I had fallen asleep, I (c) awakened by these noises. I (c) my husband who was always asleep, and we (c) all over the room trying to discover where the noise was coming from, but the parrot (c) asleep in his cage downstairs.

This mystery (d) for a year. The same thing (a) every night. I (c) the noise, I (c) my husband to get up, and we (c) to find where the noise was coming from.

One night, after I (d) the noise, I (d) the light quickly and there was my husband, squawking like a parrot! The mystery was solved. Instead of learning how to talk, our parrot had taught my husband how to squawk!

Key:
(a)—*used to*   (b)—*was/were always*   (c)—*would*   (d)—past tense

III. Write a composition on one of the following topics. Try to use *would, was always,* and *used to* whenever possible.

1. An unforgettable person you used to know.
2. A famous person from the past and some of his/her habits.
3. An eccentric relative of yours that you remember.

DISCUSSION

I. Talk about what people used to believe and what their attitudes used to be in the past. Use the following suggestions.

1. the solar system
2. witches

3. old medical practices
4. fashions
5. ancient religions
6. superstitions

II. Talk about things that you, or people you know, used to believe. Here are some examples of what people used to believe when they were children.

"I used to believe that when you turned off the TV, everything would 'freeze.' I mean—I used to think that when you turned the television on again, an hour later maybe, the actors would be doing the same things as they were when the television had been turned off."

"I used to believe that the Empire State Building was so high that it could be seen from any point in the U.S., no matter where you were."

"I used to think that there were little actors inside the TV set who performed when you turned the TV on."

BITS AND PIECES

I. Change the following using *whenever*, *whatever*, and *wherever*.

Example: Doris went somewhere; her children always went too. *Wherever Doris went, her children would always go too.*

1. I started to say something; he always interrupted me.
2. Billy did something; his little brother always did the same.
3. She went somewhere; she always took her dog.
4. She came to visit us; she always talked about her problems.
5. He went somewhere; he always took his whole family.
6. He said something; his little boy always said the same thing.
7. I watched TV; I always got a headache.
8. David went somewhere; his little dog always followed him.
9. I believed something; he always believed the same.
10. He came to visit me; he always brought me flowers.

II. Read the following story.

Monkey Business

When Rupert Forrester bought a chimpanzee to keep him company, he soon realized that he had gotten more than he expected. The monkey was more than just a monkey—it was his shadow. If he ate an apple, steak, or sandwich, the monkey pretended to do the same. If he pulled out a cigarette and lit it, the monkey imitated him. If he went to the kitchen, bathroom, or bedroom, or even outside, Corky, his little friend, followed him.

But he was truly astonished to find that the monkey was even able to reproduce his abstract drawings with precision and imitate closely every note he sang. Day after day, Corky's feats continued to astonish Rupert. When Rupert dialed a number on the phone, Corky did the same on the extension. If Rupert felt sad, his little friend would seem to suffer too.

After a month, Rupert called a friend to tell him about the monkey's astonishing abilities. "You wouldn't believe it. He imitates every single thing I do—perfectly—as if he were human. If I pick up a book, he picks one up too and pretends to read. If I turn on the radio in the living room, he turns on the one in the kitchen. If I laugh, he laughs. If I smile, he smiles. If I hide my money, he finds the place and hides his cookies there. If I light up a cigarette, cigar, or pipe, Corky pretends to do the same."

"That's fantastic!" Rupert's friend replied enthusiastically. "You've got to take him to the circus. You could make a fortune with him. He's a genius!"

Rupert grabbed Corky, dressed him, and took the next plane to New York. Outside, in the waiting room of P.T. Farnum, the great circus manager, his heart beat quickly thinking of all the money he would make from his wonderful monkey.

"Mr. Farnum will see you now," said the receptionist.

Inside the office, Rupert could not control his enthusiasm. "I've got an animal act that will make you a million—two million, no, three million dollars, Mr. Farnum."

Farnum's eyes lit up at the thought of money. "Well, let me call my secretary first. I want her to take down in shorthand everything you say. Then she can type up a report . . . and even a contract."

"Betsy, come here," Mr. Farnum called to his secretary.

Rupert's eyes popped out of his head when he turned around. There, sitting at a desk, wearing glasses and holding a steno pad and pencil in a most professional manner, was a young chimpanzee.

Using facts from the story, make statements about Rupert and Corky with *whenever, wherever, whatever*.

Examples: Whenever Rupert watched TV, Corky would do the same.
Wherever Rupert sat, Corky would sit too.
Whatever Rupert sang, Corky would sing too.

PRESENTATION

THE CARDIGANS' DAY IN COURT

Her mother, in tears, begged Joan to change her mind.

I. Read the following text and ask questions about it based on the information in italics.

Examples: *ten years ago* "When did Joan meet Vince?"
seventeen "How old was Joan at the time?"

Ten years ago, seventeen-year-old Joan Kaplin arrived home and announced to her parents that she intended to marry *Vince Cardigan,* a man she had met only *six days earlier.* Naturally, *her parents were horrified.* Her mother, in tears, begged Joan *to change her mind* and asked her *not to see Vince any more.*

Mr. Kaplin lost his temper and shouted, "You're not old enough to get married. I want you to go *to college.* We can't let you make this foolish mistake. You do *not* have my permission to marry a man you hardly know!"

When Joan insisted, he told her to *pack her bags and leave.* Joan left home *that same day* and married Vince *the next. After several unhappy months,* the couple went to court *because they found that they were totally incompatible.*

II. Take the parts of Mr. and Mrs. Cardigan and their lawyers. For your questions and answers, try to use *make, let, force, oblige, order,* and *want.* Refer to the above cues for help.

Example: MRS. CARDIGAN'S LAWYER: You say that your husband forces you to do certain things. What things?
MRS. CARDIGAN: Well, he forces me to wash the windows every day.
MRS. CARDIGAN'S LAWYER: And you say that he doesn't let you do certain things.
MRS. CARDIGAN: That's right. For instance, he doesn't let me wear bright clothes and make-up.

Expansion

I. Read the following short play aloud, taking the parts of the characters. Cast of characters: 2 attendants, 1 hijacker, 9 passengers, 2 uniformed men

The Hijacking

ATTENDANT 1: Would you like me to bring you some coffee, sir?
PASSENGER 1: No thank you, I'd rather have a martini.
ATTENDANT 2: *(to another passenger)* Would you like anything to drink, sir?
PASSENGER 2: Yes. A Scotch on the rocks, please, and soon. It'll help make the trip go faster.
HIJACKER: Miss!
ATTENDANT 1: Yes, sir?
HIJACKER: I'm a hijacker and I'm carrying a gun. I'm warning everyone here not to move! *(All the passengers scream.)*
ATTENDANT 1: Oh no! What do you want me to do?
HIJACKER: I want you to tell the pilot to change course.
PASSENGER 3: You can't do this! It's an outrage! I'm a busy man and I have to be in Paris tonight.
PASSENGER 4: And what about me? My whole family is waiting for me in Geneva! If we don't get there on time, they'll be worried.
HIJACKER: What do I care about your family? Shut up and sit down!
PASSENGER 5: Be quiet! He's dangerous! Don't make him use his gun!
ATTENDANT 1: Is there any special place you want to go, sir?
HIJACKER: I want you to take me to Pogolandia.
PASSENGER 6: I don't believe it! That madman is forcing us to go to another destination.
PASSENGER 7: But that's not possible! This is awful! What's going to happen to us?

PASSENGER 8: You can't make us change all our plans. I'm a doctor and I'm taking this man to Geneva for an operation. If he doesn't get there soon, he might die. I beg you to change your mind.

PASSENGER 9: I don't want them to take us anywhere else! I'm a sick man! I'm a sick man, do you hear? Where are my pills?

PASSENGER 4: Allow me to introduce myself. I'm a psychiatrist and I think there's something you should know—

HIJACKER: I told you to shut up and sit down! (*to attendant*) I want you to go and get the pilot, right now!

ATTENDANT 2: But sir . . . there must be some mistake. I think—

HIJACKER: Move it!

ATTENDANT 2: But sir . . . (*she leaves in frustration and comes back with two men in uniforms.*)

UNIFORMED MAN 1: What seems to be the problem here?

HIJACKER: Will you take me to Pogolandia or do you want me to use this gun?

UNIFORMED MAN 2: We can't take you to Pogolandia, sir.

HIJACKER: You can't?! You mean you're asking me to use my gun.

UNIFORMED MAN 1: No, sir.

PASSENGER 7: (*to uniformed men*) Can't you pretend to change course? He's obviously crazy, and our lives may be in danger.

UNIFORMED MAN 2: I think you've made a bad mistake, sir. This is the dining car of the 5:30 express train from Milan to Paris.

UNIFORMED MAN 1: If you want a jet plane, I'm afraid you'll have to go to the airport for that.

II. After practicing the parts several times, act out this play in class. Try to memorize your lines if possible.

GRAMMAR SUMMARY

VERBS FOLLOWED BY AN OBJECT + THE INFINITIVE

I. The following verbs take an object + the infinitive: *advise, allow, ask, force, get, oblige, order, permit, tell, want, would like.*

| I want / would like | *you to type* these letters. |

| He told / asked / advised | *the students to / not to* smoke. |

Susan's parents will never permit / allow *her to go* to that party.

What did the sergeant order / force / oblige *his men to do?*

II. The verb *get* when it means "cause," "persuade," or "force," is also used with an object and the infinitive.

Examples: The president finally got *Congress to agree* to the amendment.

Do you think you can get *your brother to fix* my car?

III. The verbs *make* and *let* are followed by an object and then the infinitive without *to.*

Examples: Some parents let *their children do* whatever they want.

They don't make *them go* to bed early.

INTENSIVE PRACTICE

I. Ask and answer questions using the cues provided. Use the simple past tense except for 7 and 10.

Example: What time _____ he _____ them _____ be   (*tell*)
there?
at 7:30
What time did he tell them to be there?
He told them to be there at 7:30.

1. What _____ the attendant _____ them _____   (*ask*)
do?
seatbelts

2. What _____ they _____ him _____ do?   (*force*)
   sign the document
3. How far _____ the sergeant _____ his men   (*make*)
   march?
   20 miles
4. When _____ he _____ her _____ marry him?   (*ask*)
   last night
5. When _____ you _____ him borrow your car?   (*let*)
   two weeks ago
6. What time _____ you _____ him _____ call   (*tell*)
   you?
   at 9:30
7. What _____ you _____ us _____ bring to the   (*would like*)
   party?
   five bags of potato chips
8. How late _____ Mr. Kline _____ his secretary   (*ask*)
   _____ work?
   until 10:00 p.m.
9. Where _____ the hijacker _____ the pilot take   (*make*)
   him?
   Pogolandia
10. How much soda _____ you _____ me _____   (*would like*)
    buy?
    three bottles

II. Ask questions based on the following statements. Your questions should
   refer to the italicized words or phrases.

Example: I want you to wait *for at least half an hour.*

          How long do you want me to wait?

1. I'd like you to wear *your new suit.*
2. Mr. Smith wants his wife to invite *seven people.*
3. They want us to be at the airport *an hour early.*
4. I'd like you to bring *a few sandwiches.*
5. I want you to meet me *in front of Reeds Bookstore.*
6. Priscilla wants Jack to wear a coat *because it's cold.*
7. Ann would like her husband to drive *a hundred more miles* before
   they stop for lunch.
8. The doctor wants Laura to lose *20 pounds.*
9. I'd like *Jack* to wash the dishes.
10. The doctor wants Laura to take her diet pills *twice a day.*

III. Change the following sentences using, *When I was a child, my parents*
   let me/didn't let me/made me/didn't make me.

Examples: I could stay up late on the weekend.
          When I was a child, my parents let me stay up late on the weekend.

          I couldn't play football after dark.
          When I was a child, my parents didn't let me play football after dark.

I had to wash the dog every weekend.
When I was a child, my parents made me wash the dog every weekend.

I didn't have to get up early on Saturdays.
When I was a child, my parents didn't make me get up early on Saturdays.

1. I had to study every evening.
2. I couldn't cross the street by myself.
3. I could only watch TV after dinner.
4. I had to clean my own room.
5. I didn't have to wash the dishes.
6. I couldn't go to the movies on week days.
7. I could go to the movies only on Saturday afternoons.
8. I had to eat all the vegetables on my plate.
9. I couldn't eat a lot of candy.
10. I had to go to school every day.
11. I didn't have to go to school when I was sick.
12. I could play with my toys.
13. I couldn't play with matches.
14. I had to read educational books.
15. I couldn't read comic books.

IV. Ask questions with *want . . . to do* and then invent appropriate answers.

Example: Ursula thinks Maria is driving too fast.
QUESTION: What does Ursula want Maria to do?
ANSWER: She wants her to drive more slowly.

1. The teacher is very angry with his students because most of them failed a recent test.
2. Mr. Jones is worried about his wife's health.
3. The Forsythes are leaving on vacation, but they're afraid that their house will be robbed in their absence. They are talking to their neighbors now.
4. Joanne is broke, and she has to pay the rent. She is talking to her rich friend now.
5. Jane doesn't know how to drive but she wants to learn. She is talking to her boyfriend now.
6. Mr. and Mrs. Wilson are talking to their son on the phone. He rarely writes to them.
7. There is a noisy party going on in apartment 302. John Bishop, who lives downstairs, is furious. He is knocking at the door of 302 now.
8. Phyllis Winston is giving Peter her phone number.
9. Mrs. Montgomery is on the phone to her family doctor. She is very worried about her son.
10. Jack thinks that Laura is so overweight that her health is suffering.

V. Make complete sentences from the following cues. Use the simple past tense and change the object into an object pronoun. Make any other necessary pronoun changes.

Example: The pilot/tell/passengers   "Keep calm and stay in your seats."
The pilot told them to keep calm and stay in their seats.

The boss/warn/employee   "Don't arrive late again."
The boss warned him not to arrive late again.

1. Margaret/ask/her husband   "Help me make the beds, all right?"
2. The thief/force/Jack and me   "Give me all your money."
3. The choral director/make/the girls   "Sing louder."
4. The lawyer/advise/Jane and Ursula   "Don't invest your money in that company."
5. She finally/get/Fred   "Sign the divorce papers."
6. Charlotte/tell/Susan   "Don't drive so fast."
7. The criminal/beg/the judge   "Don't put me in jail."
8. The teacher/allow/Janet   "Take your exam in July."
9. He/let/Dan   "Take my car."
10. Anne/make/her daughter   "Pick up your toys."

WRITING AND HOMEWORK

I. Read the following dialogue and then rewrite Ken's words using *make, let, allow, permit, force, oblige,* and *warn* where possible.

Example: Well, they made us get up at six a.m. and they forced us to line up outside the corridor. Then they allowed us to walk . . .

KEN: Yeah, they were the worst two years of my life.
ALBERT: Why?
KEN: Well, we had to get up at six a.m. and line up outside the corridor. Then we walked in single file to the dining hall where we had to wait in line for an hour or so to be served. What a sight we were in those horrible dark uniforms we had to wear! And that tasteless institutional food we had to eat! It was like eating cardboard. But the worst part was all that hard work we had to do, and we couldn't even leave for a minute to take a rest or get a drink. But the torture didn't end there. When we were back in our dormitories and they had shut off the lights, we couldn't make a sound or get out of bed. We couldn't play cards or listen to music or do anything after ten p.m.
ALBERT: Gee, Ken. You never told me you had been in prison!
KEN: Prison? I was never in prison. I'm talking about my days in an expensive boarding school!

II. After she had been married for a few months, Joan Cardigan realized that her parents had been right after all. Write a dialogue between Joan and her best friend, Lisa. She's telling her friend what her parents *wanted/told/begged/asked her to do/not to do.* You may refer to the *Presentation* on page 30 for some ideas to help you.

III. In every country there is a certain amount of bureaucracy involved in situations like
—getting a driver's license
—applying for a passport
—getting married
Write about a frustrating encounter you have had with bureaucracy, making sure to include what "they" *told/asked/wanted you to do*, and *made you do.*

DISCUSSION

I. Set up a divorce court situation in the classroom. The wife and the husband are both fighting for custody of their child. Choose a judge and divide into two groups as follows:

Wife's group	*Husband's group*
wife	husband
her best friend	his best friend
her mother	aunt
person living across the hall	person living in the apartment below
wife's lawyer	husband's lawyer
etc.	etc.

Each group should separate and plan a strategy. The issue is the custody of the child. Be prepared to present evidence showing who should or should not have custody. After both sides have "testified," the judge will hand down his decision.

II. Many strange and interesting things happen at airports and on airplanes. Act out the following situations in pairs. Then present them to the class.

1. You have arrived at your hotel in New York from the airport and discovered that you have taken another person's suitcase by mistake. The owner lives in Kansas. You telephone him to find out if he has your suitcase (he does) and you discuss arrangements for exchanging them.
2. In airports there are metal detectors which all passengers must pass through in order to show that they are not carrying weapons. In a panic, the man in front of you has put a pistol into your pocket without your knowing it. The security guard is accusing you of illegal possession of a gun. You try to convince him of your innocence.
3. You are on a plane in the "No Smoking" section. A man who couldn't find a seat in the smoking section sits next to you and starts chain smoking. You dislike this very much, but he refuses to stop smoking.
4. You are sitting near the window on a plane and you see a large, bright object near the wing. You try to convince the stewardess that you've seen a UFO, but whenever she looks out the window she sees nothing at all.

5. You are at the airport. The airline has overbooked the flight, and there is only one seat left. You are a brain surgeon who has to perform an important operation tonight. Another passenger, a detective following a dangerous international criminal, says that it is more important for him to catch the flight. You each defend your position.

BITS AND PIECES

Special use of will

I. Offers of help
Look at the following ten problems and offer to help by using *I'll . . .* and an appropriate response.

Example: The baby's crying. *I'll go and see what's wrong.*

1. The phone's ringing.
2. My suitcase is really heavy.
3. I have so much work to do.
4. I can't understand this letter. It's in French.
5. Look at all those dirty dishes.
6. I can't find my keys anywhere.
7. I don't have any money.
8. My alarm clock isn't working.
9. I have to walk all the way home.
10. My regular babysitter is sick.

II. *Won't* and *Wouldn't* for refusals
   1. *Won't*
   Mrs. Newton is complaining to her neighbor about her son, Jimmy, who refuses to cooperate.

Example: MRS. NEWTON: I keep telling him to clean up his room, but he simply refuses!
   NEIGHBOR: You mean he won't clean up his room when you tell him to?
   MRS. NEWTON: That's right. He won't do *anything* I tell him to.

Create similar dialogues between Mrs. Newton and her neighbor using the following:

—pick up his clothes   —put away his bicycle
—do his homework   —mow the lawn
—take a bath   —turn down his record player

   2. *Wouldn't*
   Wouldn't is used to express refusal in the past. Change the dialogues in Exercise 1 to the simple past tense and use *wouldn't* for the refusal.

Example: MRS. NEWTON: I kept telling him to clean up his room, but he simply refused.
   NEIGHBOR: You mean he wouldn't clean up his room when you told him to?

3. *Won't*
Complete the following using *won't* to indicate a refusal in the present.

Example: They're questioning the spy now, but he . . .
They're questioning the spy now, but he won't tell them anything.

    a. He insulted her the other day, so she . . .
    b. She failed her exams, so her parents . . .
    c. He's trying to persuade his landlord not to raise the rent, but he . . .
    d. He's afraid of dentists, so he . . .
    e. He has proposed to her several times, but she . . .

4. *Wouldn't*
Complete the following using *wouldn't* to indicate a refusal in the past.

Example: He gave her a diamond ring, but she . . .
He gave her a diamond ring, but she wouldn't accept it.

    a. I tried to talk to him calmly, but he . . .
    b. She tried to bring three bottles of Scotch through customs, but they . . .
    c. I bought a new evening dress, but my husband . . .
    d. They talked to their boss, but he . . .
    e. He wore jeans and a T-shirt to the casino, so they . . .

PRESENTATION

BREAK-IN AT THE DUBCEKS'

By the time we got there, they'd already stolen the jewels.

Judge John Dubcek was working on an important court case. He kept secret papers about the case locked in a safe at his home. The city police put a guard outside his door to protect the judge's home and family. One day while the judge and his family were out, criminals came and . . .

1. knocked the police guard out
2. tied him up and gagged him
3. turned off the alarm system
4. broke down the door
5. drugged the dog
6. went through all the rooms
7. turned the house upside down
8. messed up the drawers
9. broke open the safe
10. took the secret papers
11. stole Mrs. Dubcek's jewels
12. cut the telephone lines
13. ate everything in the refrigerator
14. left a threatening note
15. vandalized the home

I. Mr. and Mrs. Dubcek are telling a detective what they noticed when they got home. Using the above cues and the following model, take the parts of the Judge and his wife and explain what had happened by the time they arrived.

JUDGE DUBCEK: When we got home, we noticed that they had knocked the police guard out—
MRS. DUBCEK: Yes, and don't forget to tell the detective that they had tied him up and gagged him, too.

II. Make the same comments again, but this time use the passive.

JUDGE DUBCEK: When we got home, we noticed that the police guard had been knocked out—
MRS. DUBCEK: Yes, and don't forget to tell the detective that he had been tied up and gagged, too.

EXPANSION

Read the following story:

Faulks' Inn

He looked at his watch, but it was still very early. He poured himself another drink and yawned. "This is going to be a long night," he thought to himself.

*   *   *

It had all started as a joke. Connell had arrived at Faulks' Inn on Wednesday. It seemed like such a peaceful old place that he decided to stay until the weekend. On the first evening of his arrival, Connell was having a drink with some of the other guests when they began asking the owner about the history of the place. He told them the following story:

In the 1800's something very strange had happened at the inn. The owner's daughter, Julie Faulks, had mysteriously disappeared from one of the large rooms on the second floor. Everyone had been shocked by this strange disappearance, but no one had ever discovered where she had gone.

Ever since the night of the mystery, guests complained of hearing strange noises coming from the room where the girl had last been seen. Several people had also seen lights and floating white objects.

When Connell and the others heard that no one had stayed in the room since 1860, they began to laugh and make jokes, especially Connell. "Superstitious nonsense!" he laughed. "People get so frightened that their minds begin to play tricks on them."

"Everyone is at least a little superstitious," said one of the guests.

"Not me!" said Connell. "Just to show you how ridiculous this story is, *I'll* stay in that room tonight."

*   *   *

"Your friends downstairs would like to know if you'd like a cup of coffee, sir." Connell was awakened by a young woman carrying a tray.

"Yes," he replied. "All this nonsense about ghosts has made me quite sleepy."

She smiled as she poured the coffee. "Yes, I never quite understood how people could believe such things either. If you need anything else, just ring."

The next day at breakfast, Connell told the other guests about the wonderful night he had spent, and how he had never slept better in his life.

"So, nothing disturbed you?" the owner asked.

"Nothing. After the maid left, I fell asleep again."

"What maid?" the owner asked. "My wife and I are the only ones who take care of the place now."

"She looked just like the girl in that picture," said Connell, pointing to a portrait above the fireplace.

"Well, Mr. Connell, you may want to change your beliefs. That's a portrait of Julie Faulks painted in 1859."

I. Before television became popular, families used to sit by their radios in the evenings and listen to dramatizations of stories. These stories would have a narrator and other actors or actresses playing the parts of the different characters. Break into groups of five and distribute the following parts: narrator, Connell, innkeeper, a guest, Julie Faulks. Read *Faulks' Inn* as a radio drama.

II. Working in groups, make this story into a play to be acted out in class. You may add more characters (for example, more guests, the owner's wife, etc.) and create new dialogue to supplement the existing text.

GRAMMAR SUMMARY

THE PAST PERFECT TENSE

had + *past participle*

AFFIRMATIVE		INTERROGATIVE		NEGATIVE	
I You etc.	*had* already *gone.*	*Had* I you etc.	ever *been* there?	I You etc.	*hadn't thought* of it before.

I. Usage
   A. The past perfect tense is used to refer to an action that happened *before* a given past tense action.

Examples: As soon as I walked into the room, I could see that someone *had been* there
before me.

She called the police because someone *had stolen* her car.

   B. The past perfect tense is often used with adverbs of time such
   as *just, already, ever,* and *never.* They are placed between *had* and
   the past participle.

Examples: When the police arrived, the thieves *had* already *escaped.*

She *had* just *arrived* when the phone started ringing.

They were very nervous because they *had* never *flown* in a jet before.

   C. By the time. . .
   This expression followed by the simple past is often used together with the past perfect to convey the idea of delay or late-
   ness.

Examples: By the time the firemen got there, the building *had* already *burned down.*

By the time I got there, my boss *had* already *left.*

II. The past participle
   A. The past participle for regular verbs is the same as the simple
   past: base form + -*ed*. The same spelling and pronunciation rules
   apply as for the simple past tense. See *Grammar Summary,* Chapter
   1.

Examples:

Verb	Simple past tense	Past participle
work	worked	worked
live	lived	lived
study	studied	studied
stop	stopped	stopped

   B. The past participle for certain irregular verbs is the same as the
   simple past tense.

Examples:

Verb	Simple past tense	Past participle
buy	bought	bought
find	found	found
think	thought	thought
catch	caught	caught

   C. The past participle for most irregular verbs, however, is completely different from the simple past tense.

Examples:

Verb	Simple past tense	Past participle
write	wrote	written
go	went	gone
see	saw	seen
choose	chose	chosen

Notes

In speaking and informal writing, the contracted form of *had* is usually used.

Examples: I'*d* never seen such a beautiful apartment in my life.

Her boss fired her before he'*d* even read the report.

INTENSIVE PRACTICE

I. Complete the following sentences using the expression *by the time* and *get to*. Use the simple past tense and the verb provided + *already*.

Example: police/the bank/the robbers   (*escape*)
By the time the police got to the bank, the robbers had already escaped.

1. we/the station/the train	(*leave*)
2. the firemen/Main Street/the house	(*burn down*)
3. we/the restaurant/our friends	(*finish eating*)
4. he/the airport/the plane	(*take off*)
5. they/school/the lesson	(*begin*)
6. she/the office/her boss	(*leave*)
7. I/the shopping center/the stores	(*close*)
8. they/the hospital/the patient	(*die*)
9. I/the station/the ticket office	(*close*)
10. we/the bus depot/the bus	(*leave*)

II. Change the following sentences using the past perfect and *just*.

Example: Right after I left the house, I noticed that my car was gone.
I had just left the house when I noticed that my car was gone.

1. Right after we got to the beach, it started to rain.
2. Right after they went to bed, they heard a strange noise outside.
3. Right after I took off my coat, my wife came in.
4. Right after he finished eating, he began to feel sick.
5. Right after she fell asleep, the dog began to bark.
6. Right after he stepped into the shower, the phone rang.
7. Right after she put up her umbrella, the sun came out.
8. Right after she bought an insurance policy, her house caught fire.
9. Right after he started his new job, the company fired him.
10. Right after they began to eat, the baby started crying.

III. Complete the following by supplying the missing verb in the past perfect.

Example: She _____ three letters before I got there.
She had written three letters before I got there.

1. They _____ asleep before their son arrived.
2. The other guests _____ all the food before we got there.
3. A thief _____ Mrs. Bodley's money before she left the store.
4. They _____ dinner before we arrived.
5. Someone _____ a rock through the window before the police arrived.
6. They _____ their homework before their parents came home.
7. The train _____ ten minutes before the taxi arrived at the station.
8. She _____ two sedatives before the doctor arrived.
9. He _____ three glasses of wine before his guests arrived.
10. He _____ all the dishes before his wife got home.

IV. Give answers to the following questions using *had never . . . before.*

Example: Did your friend enjoy seeing the ballet?
Yes! She had never seen a ballet before.

1. Did they enjoy eating that Indian food?
2. Did you enjoy riding that horse yesterday?
3. Did Lucy like having tea with the Schmidts?
4. Did the children enjoy going to the circus?
5. Did the Mercers enjoy giving that cocktail party?
6. Did you enjoy driving John's sports car?
7. Did Grace enjoy taking Portuguese lessons?
8. Did Evelyn enjoy writing that report?
9. Did she enjoy speaking to the President?
10. Did Bob enjoy flying in that helicopter yesterday?

V. Many people insist that the most important achievements in history have taken place in the twentieth century. Others believe that many events of extraordinary importance took place even before 1500. The following dates given on the left are at least one year after the events on the right really happened.

1. 2499 B.C.—King Cheops builds the Giza pyramid and the Sphinx
2. 1762 B.C.—Hammurabi writes his code of laws
3. 751 B.C.—Romulus founds Rome
4. 440 B.C.—Phidias designs the Parthenon in Athens
5. 299 B.C.—the Mayans invent the calendar
6. 1001—Leif Ericson and the Norsemen discover the North American coast
7. 1297—Marco Polo writes a detailed account of life in China.
8. 1457—Gutenberg completes the first printed Bible
9. 1493—Christopher Columbus discovers America
10. 1498—Vasco da Gama charts a sea route to India

A. Refer to the facts and dates above and make sentences with *By the year . . .* + the past perfect and *already.*

Examples: By the year 2499 B.C. King Cheops had already built the Giza pyramid and the Sphinx.

By the year 1762 B.C. Hammurabi had already written his code of laws.

B. Refer to the facts and dates above, using *By the year . . .* + the past perfect as before. This time complete the sentence using the passive voice and omitting the agent.

Examples: By the year 2499 B.C. the Giza pyramid and the Sphinx had already been built.

By the year 1762 B.C. his code of laws had already been written.

WRITING AND HOMEWORK

I. Complete the following using the past perfect tense.

1. By the time I arrived, they _____ already _____ dinner. *(eat)*

2. Barbara _____ just _____ the house when the phone started ringing. *(leave)*

3. Longhorn Trumbolt, the author, _____ three books before he was twenty-one years old. *(write)*

4. I really enjoyed the masquerade party. I _____ never _____ to one before. *(be)*

5. When their visitors finally arrived, Mr. and Mrs. McMaster _____ already _____ to bed. *(go)*

6. By the time the police arrived, the thieves _____ already _____ the money. *(steal)*

7. Jim enjoyed his trip to Paris. He _____ never _____ in a jet plane before. *(fly)*

8. Kate _____ just _____ two sedatives when the doctor arrived. *(take)*

9. Professor Collins _____ at three American universities before accepting a position at the University of Lisbon. *(teach)*

10. By the time she finally finished talking, most of the audience _____ asleep. *(fall)*

II. A. The following dates on the left are one year after the actual event. As in Exercise V in the *Intensive Practice* section, use the facts and dates to write a sentence in the past perfect.

Examples: By the year 1536 Pizarro *had* already *conquered* Peru.

1. 1536—Pizarro conquers Peru
2. 1542—Hernando de Soto discovers the Mississippi River

3. 1589—the British defeat the Spanish Armada
4. 1605—Shakespeare writes his best plays
5. 1621—the Puritans found the Plymouth settlement
6. 1649—Shah Jehan builds the Taj Mahal
7. 1752—Benjamin Franklin discovers the principles of electricity
8. 1753—French intellectuals publish the first encyclopedia
9. 1788—the British establish their first colony in Australia
10. 1790—the electors choose George Washington as first president of the U.S.

B. Do the exercise above using the passive form of the past perfect.

Example: By the year 1536 Peru *had* already *been conquered.*

III. The following are last lines of imaginary short stories. Choose one and write a short composition to suit the ending.

1. . . . and that's why I'll never walk under a ladder again.
2. . . . and that's why I wouldn't live in that strange house if they gave it to me for free.
3. . . . so you see, the explanation of the ghost was really quite simple in the end.
4. . . . and nobody ever saw or heard from him again.
5. . . . and now I'm convinced that animals can sense danger before humans can.

DISCUSSION

I. In *Intensive Practice* V, you read that many people think that the most important achievements in history have taken place in the twentieth century. Do you believe this is true? Are the automobile, the atomic bomb, the computer, and most other things we associate with the twentieth century, positive achievements?

II. "I was in a deep sleep. Then for no reason I woke up in a panic and ran out of the house. Just as I reached the street, the roof of the building fell in. I don't really understand it, but I feel I was warned by my father who died ten years ago."

This incident, like the story of *Faulks' Inn* on page 41, suggests that the spirit world has an effect on the real world. Do you know of any similar cases, and if so do you think they have a rational explanation?

BITS AND PIECES

Might as well

The expression *might as well* is used when a person is making the best of a situation or taking full advantage of it.

Examples: I *might as well* stay home and do my homework, since I don't have enough money to go out.

He *might as well* buy the small car, since he doesn't have enough money for the big one.

Read the following short paragraphs and decide what each person might say. Use *might as well* and *since*.

Example: Mr. Harrison, the grocer, has had no customers all afternoon. In one hour it will be closing time, but he's tired now and anxious to get home.

MR. HARRISON: "I *might as well* close the store, *since* nobody has been here all afternoon."

or "I *might as well* go home early, *since* I'm kind of tired to-day."

1. Jack and Martha have to go to Akron, Ohio. They have already driven 300 miles, but Jack is still full of energy.
2. Lewis has just missed his plane to New York. There isn't another flight until tomorrow. Lewis doesn't like buses, but there is one leaving for New York in an hour.
3. It is one o'clock in the morning, but Mary can't fall asleep. She is thinking about her kitchen, which is a mess.
4. The Thompsons intended to eat Christmas dinner out. All the restaurants are closed, though, except for a small snack bar.
5. Jack has been waiting for an hour to see Dr. Connally, and he is bored. There are a few old magazines on the table in front of him that he hadn't intended to read.
6. The Johnsons' car engine doesn't work. They hadn't intended to get it fixed until they found out that a new car would cost too much.
7. The Rosses invited some people to a small dinner party at their home. The guests were supposed to arrive at eight. It is now midnight, and no one has come yet.
8. Janis needs a bottle of shampoo. She doesn't have much money, but she notices that there is a sign above her favorite shampoo that says, "Buy one and get another one for half price."
9. Harry is going to a party. There is a bottle of wine in his refrigerator that's been there for a year.
10. Donna is going to Finland for her Christmas vacation. She wanted to buy a new winter coat before she went, but she knows she can get one in Finland for half the price.
11. Jack wanted to send his brother a telegram for his birthday, but he

found out that a telegram would only be two dollars cheaper than a phone call.

12. Mary was going to throw out an old pair of shoes until she saw in the latest fashion magazine that the shoes were in style again.

13. The Suskinds want to go to a movie, but nothing good is playing. They remember that there is an old Bogart film on television to-night.

14. Florence is in a nice hot shower. She wasn't planning to wash her hair, but the water feels so good.

6

PRESENTATION

ASK THE EXPERTS

I'm embarrassed to take my brother Herman anywhere!

The following letters appeared in newspaper advice columns:

Amy Post's Problem Corner

AMY POST

Dear Amy:

I'm embarrassed to take my brother Herman anywhere. At a restaurant one day he ordered chicken and *began to eat it with his fingers.* At the same meal, *he drank his soup from the bowl, talked constantly with his mouth full, cleaned his hands and mouth on the tablecloth,* and *drank his Coca-Cola from the bottle.*

When I told him he didn't have any manners, he laughed and said that formal manners were a thing of the past. Please answer my letter and tell him how he should act in public.

Sister of a Slob

I. Ask and answer questions with *should* (or *ought to* only in the affirmative) about the letter you have just read. Your questions should relate to the italicized phrases.

Example:
A: Do you think people should eat chicken with their fingers?
B: People shouldn't eat chicken with their fingers in a restaurant, but I suppose that at a picnic it's all right.

II. Are formal manners a thing of the past? Give your opinions.

Ask Doctor Walters

DR. WALTERS

Dear Dr. Walters:

I'm writing to ask your advice, since my wife has refused to see a doctor. She suffers terribly from insomnia and sometimes gets only *three or four hours of sleep a night.*

She is the executive director of a company and she has to make a lot of important decisions every day. She sometimes *works twelve hours a day, smokes three packs of cigarettes,* and *often misses lunch.* Even though she arrives home exhausted, she still finds time to *make dinner* and *clean the house.* She insists on *doing everything herself.*

I'm convinced that her demanding life is the cause of her insomnia, but she disagrees and keeps on taking *stronger doses of sleeping pills.* What should I do?

Desperate Husband

I. Ask and answer questions about the above letter. Use *should* (or *ought to* only in the affirmative). Your questions should refer to the italicized phrases.

Example:
A: How many hours should people sleep a night?
B: People should/ought to sleep at least eight hours a night.

II. Suggest what "Desperate Husband" can do to help his wife.

You and Your Child
by Millicent Mildew

MILLICENT MILDEW

Dear Millicent:

Help! My wife and I don't agree about how we should raise our child, and it's ruining our marriage. She is very strict and *makes Johnny study for three hours* when he comes home from school, *eat everything on his plate,* as well as *help with the housework. She refuses to let him watch television* at all, and she is a firm believer in *physical punishment.*

I say that childhood is a time for playing, that TV expands a child's vocabulary, that children should have no homework, that a child should eat only what he feels like eating, and that physical punishment is medieval. What should I do?

A Worried Father

I. Ask and answer questions about the above letter. Use *should* (or *ought to* only in the affirmative). Your questions should relate to the italicized phrases.

Example:

A: Should parents make their children study after school?

B: I think children should/ought to study after school if they are having trouble with their work. But three hours is perhaps too much.

II. Do you think differences of opinion on how to raise a child can ruin a marriage? How should children be raised?

The Heart Line
by Martha Gold

MARTHA GOLD

Dear Martha:

At a recent international medical conference in Lisbon, I met a very kind, intelligent man who is *divorced and has three children.* We fell in love and intend to get married. I can see, though, that we are going to have a lot of problems since I am *American and he is European.*

I am a *doctor with a successful practice in New York, and he has his own practice in Europe.* We manage to communicate reasonably well, but *in French, which is neither my native language, nor his.* To make matters worse, *we do not share the same political beliefs.*

Although we love each other deeply, I'm afraid that these cultural barriers along with professional and family problems will ruin our chances for a stable marriage. What should we do?

A Concerned Doctor

I. Ask and answer questions about the above letter. Use *should* (or *ought to* only in the affirmative). Your questions should relate to the italicized phrases.

Example:

A: Should a divorced person with three children marry again?

B: Sure. I think that he or she should marry again, as long as his or her children like the new partner.

II. What are the possible obstacles to the success of the marriage of the two people in the above letter? Do you think their marriage will succeed? Do you know of any marriages where the partners are of different nationalities? Do they have any problems?

EXPANSION

Vacation Tips

The following panel discussion is taking place on a television program called *TV Journal.* Read it and take the parts of the different characters.

REPORTER 1: In a few weeks, a lot of families will be packing their bags and leaving for their annual vacations. We have with us tonight five officers of the State Police and a special guest with a few suggestions for all you vacationers who may be watching. Officer Russell, what is the first thing people should do before going on vacation?

OFFICER RUSSELL: People who plan to drive their cars should have a tune-up done at their local garage, to be sure that everything is working properly.

OFFICER WEINSTEIN: Yes. These safety checks are inexpensive and could save a lot of time and trouble later on.

REPORTER 2: What should people do to protect their houses or apartments while they are gone?

OFFICER DIANGELO: In order to discourage burglars, who usually prefer to rob empty houses, families should cancel all deliveries of milk, newspapers, and mail. They should also ask their neighbors to check the house occasionally.

OFFICER BROWN: You know, some authorities say that a light ought to be left on, as if someone were home, but this could be expensive and even dangerous if the vacationers plan to be away for a long time. I think that people should perhaps leave some of their blinds up, to give the house a less "closed" look.

REPORTER 1: When people are enjoying themselves on vacation, they are often less careful with their money and belongings, isn't that so?

OFFICER MERCIER: This is very true. People also tend to be carrying a lot more money than usual. First of all, vacationers ought to buy traveler's checks instead of carrying cash. They should avoid carrying a lot of money, and all baggage should be locked in the trunk of the car where it can't be seen.

LEFTY EVANS: I think it's important to remember that people should leave valuable items such as cameras and suitcases in their cars. They ought to leave their cars far away from campsites, especially in deserted areas. Families should also let mail accumulate in mail boxes. Men should carry their wallets in outside pockets, and most important of all, people shouldn't leave any animals on guard outside their homes.

REPORTER 2: Hey! Wait a minute! That sounds like bad advice to me. You don't seem to know what you're talking about.

OFFICER WEINSTEIN: He *should* know! Lefty just got out of jail for burglary and pickpocketing. What he says is very good advice—if people follow it in reverse!

I. What should people who are going on vacation remember to do?

II. Imagine that this panel discussion has been conducted with a group of burglars instead of police officers. Create your own discussion in the classroom.

GRAMMAR SUMMARY

Should/Ought to

I. *Should* (+ base form) and *ought to* (+ base form) are most commonly used when giving and asking for advice. The passive *should be* (+ past participle) and *ought to be* (+ past particple) are commonly used when the speaker is expressing an opinion.

ACTIVE	PASSIVE
I | should | pay the telephone bill / ought to | soon.	Children | should be | seen and not / ought to be | heard.
I think you | should | see a doctor / ought to | soon.	I think drunk drivers | should be | / ought to be | / punished.
Should(n't) | I call the fire department?	Should(n't) | that man be taken to the hospital?
Do(n't) you think I | should | buy / ought to | / a new car?	Do(n't) you think she | should be | made / ought to be | / a vice president?
You | shouldn't | smoke so much.	Teenagers | shouldn't be | allowed to smoke.
I don't think you | should | see that / ought to | film.	I don't think children | should be | / ought to be | / spoiled.

II. Whereas *should* may be used in the affirmative, interrogative, and negative, in American English *ought to* is usually used in the affirmative only. The interrogative and negative of *ought to* can be formed, however, with the verb *think*.

Examples: Incorrect: He oughtn't to go.
Correct: I don't think he ought to go

Incorrect: Oughtn't you to call the police?
Correct: Don't you think you ought to call the police?

Notes

i. Always remember that *should* is never followed by *to*.

ii. It is the verb *think* that is always in the negative form when used with *should* or *ought to* in a negative or negative-interrogative sentence.

Examples: I don't think you |should |go out tonight.
                              |ought to |

Don't you think you |should |study harder?
                               |ought to |

INTENSIVE PRACTICE

I. Use *do you think* and *should* to complete the following.

Example: What _____ I _____ do?
What do you think I should do?

1. When _____ we _____ buy the tickets?
2. What _____ I _____ wear?
3. How much _____ I _____ take out of the bank?
4. How much weight _____ I _____ lose?
5. Where _____ they _____ meet us?
6. What time _____ I _____ be there?
7. Where _____ we _____ spend our vacation?
8. Which newspaper _____ I _____ buy?
9. Who _____ I _____ invite to the party?
10. Which restaurant _____ we _____ go to?

II. Use both *don't you think you should* and *shouldn't you,* and give advice for the following.

Example: I'm going to borrow Bill's car.

Don't you think you should ask him first?

Shouldn't you ask him first?

1. I've been feeling sick for two weeks.
2. I have an exam tomorrow, but I think I'll go to a party tonight.
3. My best friend hasn't told his fiancée that he spent ten years in prison.
4. My electricity bill came two weeks ago.
5. I think someone stole my wallet while I was waiting for the bus.
6. My plane leaves in 45 minutes. I think I'll take a bus to the airport.
7. My passport expired last week.
8. If the train doesn't arrive in ten minutes, I'm going home.
9. I can't see very clearly anymore. I've had three car accidents this month.
10. I think I'll ask my boss for a $5,000 raise.

III. Rewrite the following using *there ought to be.*

Example: There's no stop sign on Elm Street.
There ought to be a stop sign on Elm Street.

1. There is no guard protecting the embassy.
2. There are no laws against drunk driving.
3. There are no street lights on that corner.
4. There is no parking space for the handicapped.
5. There is no light in the hall.
6. There is no pension for old people.
7. There is only one way to get out of the building.
8. There are no fire exits in that movie theater.
9. There's no fire department in that town.
10. There's no fine for littering in that city.

IV. Use *should* and *ought to* to give your opinions on the following.
Begin: I think _____ should/ought to _____ *or* I don't
think _____ should/ ought to _____ .

Example: people/money to beggars
I think people ought to give money to beggars.
or   *I don't think people should give money to beggars.*

1. men/their wives with the housework
2. people/the dentist twice a year
3. children/permitted/violent TV programs
4. people/hitchhikers
5. children/physically punished

V. Match the items on the left with the descriptions on the right according
to your personal beliefs. Use *should* in the passive. Be ready to give
reasons for your opinions.

Example: As far as I am concerned, *examinations* should be *compulsory/*
abolished/voluntary because . . .

examinations	severely punished
military service	compulsory
violent sports	pardoned
capital punishment	permitted
juvenile delinquents	imprisoned
alcoholics	treated by a psychiatrist
drunk drivers	abolished
smoking in public places	fined
hijackers	voluntary

WRITING AND HOMEWORK

I. Complete the following sentences using *should* or *ought to*.

1. You _____. If not, you'll probably fail your exam.
2. Don't you think you _____? It's raining very hard.
3. I don't think you _____. Too much coffee might keep you awake.
4. I think you _____. The hotels might all be full.
5. You _____. You'll get a terrible sunburn.
6. I don't think you _____. It's against the law, you know.
7. Don't you think you _____? Your clothes don't fit you any more.
8. I don't think you _____. The baby might wake up.
9. You _____. The neighbors might complain.
10. I don't think you _____. Your wife will get terribly upset.

II. Give an opinion about the following topics, using *should* or *ought to*.

Example: sex education in schools

Sex education ought to be taught in schools because qualified specialists can answer children's questions about relationships between men and women.

or   Sex education shouldn't be taught in school. It is the parents' responsibility to inform children about sex.

or   Parents should protest against sex education in schools because it is the parents' responsibility to inform their children about sex.

or   Parents should encourage sex education in schools. Doctors and nurses working with the school system are better qualified than parents to answer children's questions.

1. sex education in schools
2. problem children
3. cheating on exams
4. people who overeat
5. sick old people
6. murderers
7. organized crime
8. homeless animals
9. heavy smokers
10. people with heart conditions
11. teachers who hit their students

III. Gloria asked Joanne to buy her a lottery ticket last Wednesday. Joanne bought two, one for herself and one for her friend. Both women forgot about the tickets until a week later when Joanne discovered that one of the tickets contained the winning number. The prize was five thousand dollars. What should she do?
1. Explain what you think Joanne should do and give reasons for your opinion.
2. Write a dialogue between Joanne and Gloria.

DISCUSSION

I. Kenneth Jackson found a wallet the other day full of twenty-dollar bills. There was no identification in the wallet, so he couldn't possibly return it to the owner. Being an indecisive person, he asked several people what he should do. Each person gave him different advice.

—His brother told him to spend the money as soon as possible, as this was a "once in a lifetime" opportunity.
—Reverend Brown advised him to give the money to charity, since many poor people would benefit.
—His boss told him to go to the police, since it would be illegal to do anything else.
—His wife advised him to keep the money and wait for an ad in the newspaper.
—A friend of his said that he should put an ad in the paper, in the "lost and found" section.

1. Discuss in groups or as a class which solution is best for this situation.
2. Each person in the class should take the part of one of Kenneth's friends or relatives and argue with him, trying to persuade him to accept a certain solution.

II. Organize a discussion based on *Vacation Tips* in the *Expansion* section. Work in groups or as a class and choose from the following topics:

—the problems of old people
—smoking
—the advantages and disadvantages of TV
—hitchhiking
—a topic of your choice

BITS AND PIECES

Supposed to

The present tense of the verb *be* with *supposed to* is usually employed when informing someone of normal or correct procedure.

Examples: You're not supposed to park here.

You're supposed to wear a tie to the casino.

The past tense of the verb *be* with *supposed to* is often used when someone has forgotten to do something.

Examples: You were supposed to call him yesterday.

You were supposed to bring all your documents.

John Howard's Wedding

Mrs. Dewhurst didn't want her daughter Agnes to marry John Howard. "He's an idiot!" Mrs. Dewhurst complained.

Her suspicions of John were confirmed on the wedding day when John showed up for the wedding wearing blue jeans and a sweater. The wedding had been set for 10:00 a.m., and John got there at 11:00. He forgot to shake the guests' hands, and said, "Yeah, sure!" instead of "I do" when it was his turn to speak. He also stood up instead of kneeling, didn't repeat the marriage vows after the priest, and walked up the aisle behind the bride instead of beside her. What's more, he forgot to order the limousine, bring the marriage certificate, and kiss the bride. He put the ring on the bride's thumb instead of on her fourth finger.

At the reception things got even worse. John danced with everyone except the bride, drank too much champagne, and forgot to cut the wedding cake.

John's mother-in-law is informing him of what he did incorrectly.

Examples: "You're supposed to wear a tuxedo to a wedding, not blue jeans and a sweater, you idiot!" she said.

"And you were supposed to shake the guests' hands, too," she added.

Continue her criticisms using *you are supposed to . . .* when referring to John's ignorance of correct procedure, and *you were supposed to . . .* when referring to John's forgetfulness.

PRESENTATION

SPOT THE DANGERS

If his mother doesn't catch him, he'll fall out of the window!

HOSPITAL   **HOME**

I. There are a lot of potential dangers in the above pictures. Can you spot them?

II. Using *if . . . will* or *if . . . won't,* discuss the dangers in the two pictures.

Examples: If he doesn't take his medicine, │he'll get worse.
          │he won't get better.

If the child leans out of the window any farther, he'll fall.

If his mother doesn't come soon, he'll fall out of the window.

EXPANSION

I. Hank, Rick, Janet, Mike, and Angela are about to rob their first bank. Right now they are outside the bank discussing potential problems. Read the following play, taking the parts of the different characters.

The Bank Job

HANK: Now, remember, gang, if we're not careful, the bank camera will take our picture. Also, the alarm will go off, and the whole neighborhood will wake up.

RICK: Not only that! As soon as it goes off, the whole New York Police Department will be here in three minutes!

JANET: Well, maybe we shouldn't go in through the front door as we planned. Let's try the side window.

MICKEY: But hold on a minute! As soon as we break in through the side window, the camera will take our pictures.

ANGELA: If we have our masks on we won't be recognized.

HANK: Okay, so our big problem is to disconnect the alarm. That's what we ought to do first. If we don't do that, we won't be able to do anything else.

RICK: I'm really scared, though. If the alarm goes off, the police will arrive right away.

JANET: And if the getaway car isn't waiting outside, they'll catch every one of us.

MICKEY: Yeah, and if they catch us, we won't get out of jail for at least ten years.

ANGELA: Hey! If they put me in jail for ten years, by the time I get out I'll be forty!

(ALL): Me too!

JANET: Why don't we all look for jobs instead?

II. Create sentences related to the above text. Use the following cues to make your sentences.

Examples: if/alarm/the noise

If the alarm goes off the noise will wake everyone up.

or   If we don't disconnect the alarm the noise will wake everyone up.

1. if/careful/bank camera
2. as soon as/alarm/New York Police Department
3. when/alarm/the whole neighborhood
4. as soon as/the side window/the camera
5. if/masks/recognized
6. if/getaway car/every one of us
7. if/to jail/for at least ten years
8. if/for ten years/forty years old

GRAMMAR SUMMARY

THE FIRST CONDITIONAL

Present Clause + Future Clause

The verb in the *if/when/as soon as* clause is in the *present tense;* the verb in the main clause is in the *future tense.*

Affirmative: If (When, As soon as) I get to Australia, I'll send you a postcard.
Interrogative: If she telephones, will you please give her this message?
Negative: If he hurries, he won't be late.

I. The "first conditional" with *if* illustrates a cause/effect relationship.

Example: If he goes swimming after he eats, he'll get sick.
        (cause)   (effect)

             If he doesn't come soon, he'll miss the bus.
                (cause)   (effect)

II. *When* and *as soon as* are followed by the present tense. The main clause is in the future tense.

Examples: When she arrives, I'll tell her the news.

             As soon as she gets home, she'll call you.

Notes

i. The order of the two clauses can usually be inverted.

Examples: If he drinks any more coffee, he'll stay awake all night.
             He'll stay awake all night if he drinks any more coffee.

             As soon as she gets home, I'll let you know.
             I'll let you know as soon as she gets home.

ii. The pronoun + *will* is usually contracted in spoken English and in informal writing.

Examples: I'll, you'll, he'll, etc.

iii. Although still used in some forms of British English, the first person *shall* is practically never used for expressing the future in American English.

iv. When the *if/when/as soon as* clause comes first, it is set off by a comma from the rest of the sentence.

INTENSIVE PRACTICE

I. The expression *What if* is used when the speaker wants to present a problem. Answer the following *What if* questions using the cues provided.

Example: What if it rains Saturday?   (we _____ the beach on Sunday)
If it rains Saturday, we'll go to the beach on Sunday.

What if they don't bring enough sandwiches?   (we _____ fruit)
If they don't bring enough sandwiches, we'll eat fruit.

1. What if we fail the exam?   (we _____ it again in June)

2. What if he has an accident?   (we _____ him to the hospital)

3. What if they run out of gas?   (they _____ to the nearest gas station)

4. What if they cancel our flight?   (we _____ the train)

5. What if the restaurant is closed?   (I _____ somewhere else)

6. What if they raise the price of gas?   (we _____ a smaller car next year)

7. What if he doesn't like liver?   (he _____ a steak)

8. What if they don't come on time?   (we _____ to the theater without them)

9. What if the dress doesn't fit her?   (she _____ another one)

10. What if he doesn't hear his alarm clock?   (he _____ late for work)

II. Change the following sentences to the negative.

Examples: If he asks her age, she'll be insulted.
If he doesn't ask her age, she won't be insulted.

If we rob the bank, we'll go to prison.
If we don't rob the bank, we won't go to prison.

1. If he passes his test, he'll get his diploma.
2. If we hurry, we'll get there on time.
3. If they bring a bottle, we'll have enough to drink.
4. If he smokes, his cough will get worse.
5. If you get here soon, the doctor will be able to see you.
6. If she sees the film, she'll be able to tell us about it.
7. If Arnold gets here soon, we'll have enough time to visit the museum.
8. If the heater works, we'll be warm enough.
9. If you study hard, you'll do well on the test.
10. If he comes soon, he'll be able to have lunch with us.

III. Comment on sentence A using *as soon as* + the present tense, and then the future tense in the main clause. Use the cues provided to formulate your comments.

Examples: A. Henry will come home soon.
    B. As soon as *he comes home, we'll tell him* about the accident.

    A. Jane and Martin will get here soon
    B. As soon as *they get here, we'll show them* their new room.

    1. A. Mark will get here soon.
        B. As soon as ―――――― the good news.
    2. A. Jane will arrive soon.
        B. As soon as ―――――― the birthday present.
    3. A. Frank and Margaret will phone soon.
        B. As soon as ―――――― the message.
    4. A. Louisa will graduate soon.
        B. As soon as ―――――― a telegram of congratulations.
    5. A. The boss will get here soon.
        B. As soon as ―――――― for a raise.
    6. A. Grandfather will come soon.
        B. As soon as ―――――― to see his new granddaughter.
    7. A. Aunt Harriet will arrive soon.
        B. As soon as ―――――― the money we owe her.
    8. A. Ted and Jack will get here soon.
        B. As soon as ―――――― to the new opera house.
    9. A. Anne and John will get married soon.
        B. As soon as ―――――― a new vacuum cleaner.
    10. A. Teresa will come back soon.
        B. As soon as ―――――― the bad news.

IV. Match the *if* clause on the left with a clause on the right. There are *several* possible combinations. First find the most logical match for each *if* clause.

Example: If my little cousin comes to visit, I'll take her to the zoo.

Now, try to find funnier possibilities for each.

Example: If my little cousin comes to visit, I'll join the navy.

If my mother-in-law comes to visit	I'll move to another city
If I can't find an apartment here	she'll bite the mailman
If my wife has twins	I'll take her to the zoo
If my boss doesn't give me a raise	I'll go out and celebrate
If Uncle Harry leaves me his fortune	I'll quit my job
If my dog gets free	I'll look for somebody else to marry
If my little cousin comes to visit	I'll go crazy
If you don't marry me	I'll call an ambulance
If Tom gets sick again	I'll call a mechanic
If my car breaks down again	I'll join the navy

V. A father and son are making New Year's resolutions together. They are both promising to do or not to do certain things if the other also promises. Take the parts of the father and son, using the "bad habit" cues.

Example: SON: If you don't lose your temper, I'll clean my room.
FATHER: If you don't play your records loud, I won't make you study on the weekend.

Bad Habits

Father	*Son*
loses his temper	doesn't clean his room
makes his son study on the week-ends	plays his records loud
	comes home late
interrupts his son's phone calls	doesn't study
insults his son's girlfriends	hits his younger sister
doesn't let him see horror movies	doesn't help his mother
doesn't lend him the car	plays ball in the living room
doesn't take him camping	smokes
doesn't help him with his math	wears dirty jeans to school
calls him an idiot	takes money without asking
goes on long business trips	doesn't eat his vegetables
wears his son's sport shirts	

WRITING AND HOMEWORK

I. Complete the following sentences with appropriate clauses.

1. If _____, we won't go to the beach.
2. If he loses his job, _____.
3. As soon as the baby is born, _____.
4. If _____, I'll call the police.
5. She _____ when she goes to Japan next month.
6. He _____ as soon as he finishes his work.
7. I'll go to the doctor next week if _____.
8. If the train arrives late, _____.
9. He'll lose his job if he _____.
10. If you don't study, _____.

II. Mr. Springer and his son Mike are talking about Mike's studies. Using the first conditional, make the following dialogue into a chain dialogue. Use the last part of each line to form the first part of the next line. Begin the dialogue like this:

Example: MIKE: But Dad! Why do I have to study?
MR. SPRINGER: If you study, you'll get good marks on your exams.
MIKE: That's right. If I get good marks on my exams, . . .

MIKE: But dad! Why do I have to study?

MR. SPRINGER: Well, don't you want to get good marks on your exams?

MIKE: That's right, and then maybe I can go to Harvard.

MR. SPRINGER: Just think! My own son, a graduate of one of the best universities in the country.

MIKE: And Dad, you know, Harvard graduates often go into politics. Maybe I will too.

MR. SPRINGER: Yes, Mike. I can see it all now. My son—with a seat in the Senate!

MIKE: Sure! And after the Senate, who knows? How does this sound, Dad? Mike Springer—President!

MR. SPRINGER: Just think! Then you can abolish education!

III. Write a letter to a friend inviting him to visit you. Talk about some of the things you will do *if/when/as soon as* he comes. Advise him as to the best means of transportation, early booking, traveler's checks, and clothes to bring. Promise to meet him when he arrives. Use *if/when/as soon as* wherever possible.

DISCUSSION

I. The illustration on page 59 shows some of the disadvantages of having a large family. Imagine that your government has passed a law that prohibits a couple from having more than two children. What are the advantages and disadvantages of such a law?

II. The illustration on page 59 also shows what a hospital stay can be like. Everyone has been either a patient or a visitor in a hospital. Let's see what some visitors, patients, and doctors have to say:

1. VISITOR 1: "In the hospitals in my country, visiting privileges are unlimited. So hundreds of noisy visitors crowd the wards at all hours of the day. Nothing is worse for patients who need rest."

VISITOR 2: "In my country patients are allowed to have only two visitors at a time, for only two hours a day. Nothing is worse for a patient than feeling alone and abandoned in a strange hospital."

2. DOCTOR 1: "What I hate most is having husbands present when their wives are giving birth. We never know how the husband is going to react, and besides, his presence distracts hospital personnel who are trying to do their job."

DOCTOR 2: "The old practice of excluding the husband is based more on tradition than on common sense. Husbands should be witnesses to a process they have helped to create. They are the people who can best help and encourage their wives at this time."

3. PATIENT 1: "I don't know why I let them put me in the hospital. I would have had better care at home. The nurses were cold, mechan-

ical, and never came when you called. The main problem is they just don't care about the patients they work with."

PATIENT 2: "I've never seen such competent, hardworking professionals in my life as nurses. Of course, they can't be at your side every minute of the day with all the patients they have to look after. They must care about their patients or why else would they have studied for years and chosen such an exhausting profession that pays so little?"

Discuss these comments by visitors, patients, and doctors, adding your own opinions to the discussion.

BITS AND PIECES

I. *What if . . . ?*

As you saw in Exercise 1 of the *Intensive Practice* section, the expression *What if* + the present or simple past tense is used when the speaker wants to point out a possible problem.

Mrs. Harris is very worried about her only child, Robert, who is going on his first trip to Europe. She is talking about possible problems to her husband, who is trying to calm her down. Some of the things that are worrying her are: Robert's plane trip, finding his way around in Europe, his hotel, money, food, the language barrier, possible illness, and letters to the family.

Taking the parts of Mrs. Harris and her husband, use *What if* + the present tense when posing the problem, and the first conditional when giving a solution.

Examples: MRS. HARRIS: What if Robert misses his plane?
MR. HARRIS: Robert can take care of himself. If he misses his plane, he'll catch the next one.
MRS. HARRIS: And what if he gets air sick?
MR. HARRIS: If he gets air sick, he'll ask the flight attendant for a pill.

II. *No wonder*

The expression *No wonder* is used to express surprise upon discovering the cause of something. There are very few phrases that have the same meaning as *no wonder;* however, *It's not surprising that* is perhaps the closest in meaning.

Example: No wonder he had an accident! He was driving at a hundred miles an hour.

(It's not surprising that he had an accident! He was driving at a hundred miles an hour.)

Use the expression *No wonder* + the past tense in the following sentences. The first eight sentences are in the affirmative, the last eight in the negative.

Examples: _____! Your window was wide open all night!

No wonder you caught a cold! Your window was wide open all night!

_____! She didn't study at all.

No wonder she didn't pass the test! She didn't study at all.

1. _____!   She shot him three times.
2. _____!   He spent half the night in the pouring rain.
3. _____!   He got up an hour late.
4. _____!   The fish he ate was a week old.
5. _____!   The electrical wiring was at least fifty years old.
6. _____!   They let him cross the street by himself.
7. _____!   They let him play with matches.
8. _____!   She forgot to take a road map.
9. _____!   He broke his leg yesterday.
10. _____!   Liver is the dish they hate the most.
11. _____!   He wasn't wearing his glasses.
12. _____!   The movie was in French, and they don't speak a word of French.
13. _____!   She was listening to records with the bedroom door closed.
14. _____!   His telephone was broken.
15. _____!   There wasn't a post office in the town where they were staying.
16. _____!   He discovered she was engaged to another man.

PRESENTATION

NUMEROLOGY

Eights love arguing and accepting challenges.

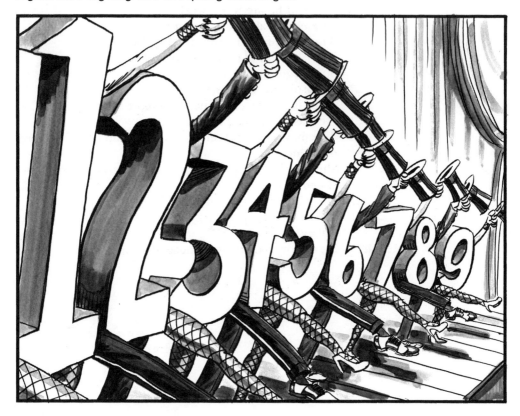

I. The occult science of numerology has been practiced for hundreds of years. Numerologists say that we can discover the secrets of our personalities by finding our "personal number." You can find your number by using the letters of your name. In the chart below, find the numerical value for each letter in your name. Then add all the numbers together. If the number you arrive at has one digit, that is your personal number. If the number you arrive at has more than one digit, add *those* digits together until you have a one-digit number. That is *your* personal number.

Numerical Values for Letters							
1	2	3	4	5	6	7	8
A	B	C	D	E	U	O	F
I	K	G	M	H	V	Z	P
Q	R	L	T	N	W		
J		S			X		
Y							

Examples: L U I S   S A N T O S   B O R G E S
3+6+1+3 + 3+1 +5+4+7+3 + 2+7+2+3+5+3 = 58
5+8 = 13
1+3 = 4
Luis's personal number is 4.

M A R Y   J A N E   R O B I N S O N
4+1+2+1 + 1+1+5+5 + 2+7+2+1+5+3+7+5 = 52
5+2 = 7
Mary Jane's personal number is 7.

Meanings of Your Personal Number

Ones enjoy being leaders and insist on having their own way in a group. They love taking on responsibilities. They are often criticized for being domineering and vain and rarely admit being wrong. Ones are ambitious and never stop trying to reach their goals.

Sensitive and sentimental, twos can't help feeling depressed when someone hurts them. Shy and reserved, they avoid talking about themselves. They are true friends, hard workers, and traditionalists. They miss not having the protection and security they had as children. Home-loving twos usually feel like spending time with their families and prefer being at home to being at a party.

"What's the use of crying?" is the motto of number three. Lively and optimistic, threes usually think first of having fun and going to parties. They love telling jokes and they are usually the most frank and popular people in the group. But threes have trouble saving money, and because of their generosity, have difficulty in managing the practical aspects of life.

Fours are ruled by a sense of duty and punctuality. They never put off writing a letter or doing a job. They never avoid doing necessary tasks. Fours always finish what they have started, and never think of doing a job they can't complete. Precise and methodical, fours insist on getting a job done perfectly and on time. They never consider having fun when there is work to do.

Restless and impatient, fives never stop looking for new experiences. They rarely finish doing a job before they start working on another one. Fives love excitement and look forward to starting new projects. Fives' love of adventure and change often prevents them from getting involved with people. They often deny feeling love for people they are close to.

Sixes are sensitive, loving, and artistic. The typical six enjoys spending time in museums, and loves reading good books and listening to good music. They hate getting into arguments and fighting. Sixes, with their loving nature, can't help trusting people and creating a sense of balance and harmony around themselves.

Sevens are often accused of being non-conformists and dreamers. They like wearing strange clothes and avoid doing what most other people do. Criticized for being radical, sevens fight for their goals and have trouble understanding conservative ideas. Sevens are deep and philosophical, and because of this, have trouble getting to know people.

Adventure, action, and excitement characterize eights. Most eights can't recall having a boring day. They are impulsive and love arguing, fighting and accepting challenges. Eights play to win and often hurt others, but they never apologize for hurting other people's feelings. They don't quit fighting until they have reached their goals.

Nines are intellectuals and humanists. They insist on reading only the best books and they never avoid helping friends who are in trouble. They keep on telling people that humanity is basically good, but they can't stand talking to people who are boring. Nines look forward to living in a peaceful world ruled by intelligence and harmony.

II. Take turns asking each other questions based on your personal numbers. Use the information provided above, and answer truthfully!

Example: STUDENT A: What's your personal number?
STUDENT B: One.
STUDENT A: Do you enjoy being a leader?
STUDENT B: No, actually I'm a very shy person.
STUDENT A: Do you always insist on having your own way?
STUDENT B: Well, I'm very stubborn. I insist on having my way in a lot of things.

EXPANSION

Read the following short story.

The Hitchhiker

John Henderson was driving home late last night from an exhausting business trip. He had put off visiting the company's new headquarters in order to get home before midnight, and now he was having trouble staying awake. He turned up the radio and tried to concentrate on the news—something about a robbery—but his eyes kept on closing. His wife was back home in Dayton, and he missed having her company on this long trip.

It was then that he noticed the hitchhiker at the side of the road. Without even thinking about what he was doing, he slowed down and stopped the car. He couldn't help feeling sorry for the young man who looked so wet and miserable in the rain. "Get in," he said.

John remembered having to hitchhike home from the university before he had a car. He couldn't stand sitting at the side of the road for hours, waiting for rides.

The hitchhiker got in and immediately John was sorry that he had picked him up. The young man had a strange face and very penetrating eyes. His clothes were old and dirty, and his long hair needed cutting. The hitchhiker lit a cigarette and said that he was going to Woodsville but when John asked him other questions, the young man avoided giving him any personal information and changed the subject.

John began to sweat and his thoughts turned nervously to his wallet and all the money he was carrying. He desperately tried to remember what the newscaster had said earlier about a robbery. Don't be ridiculous! he thought to himself. Stop imagining things! This guy isn't a criminal. What's the use of panicking?

Even though he had quit smoking three months before, John felt like having a cigarette. He asked his passenger for one but before lighting it, he had to wait for his hands to stop shaking. At the next small town John stopped the car and said, "I just can't seem to stay awake. I think I'll try and find a hotel and spend the night here." He apologized nervously to the hitchhiker for not being able to drive him to Woodsville.

The young man slowly reached into his pocket. "This is it!" thought John. "I'm a dead man." At that very moment he considered shouting for help, but instead of a gun or a knife, the hitchhiker pulled out several wrinkled bills and offered them to John. "Oh, no. I don't want your money. Just get out, Okay?"

The young man looked puzzled, but insisted on giving John the money—$500. "My father is John Baresford, the oil millionaire, you see," he said. "Thanks for taking me this far."

John waited until his passenger had disappeared from sight, then he stepped on the gas and drove out of town. He was looking forward to getting home. Martha will never believe this! he thought to himself.

I. According to the text, the following statements are wrong. Correct them, using the cues provided.

Example: John visited the company's new headquarters.   *No. He put off . . .*
No. He put off visiting the company's new headquarters.

1. It was easy for him to stay awake that night.   *No. He had trouble . .*
2. His eyes were wide open.   *No. His eyes kept on . . .*
3. He didn't like having his wife's company.   *No. He missed . . .*
4. He didn't feel sorry for the young man.   *No. He couldn't help . . .*
5. He forgot about having to hitchhike as a student   *No. He remembered . . .*
6. He used to like waiting at the side of the road.   *No. He couldn't stand . . .*
7. The hitchhiker's hair was short.   *No. His hair needed . . .*
8. The young man freely gave personal information.   *No. He avoided . . .*
9. John had started smoking three months before.   *No. He had quit . . .*
10. John didn't say anything about not driving the young man to Woodsville.   *No. He apologized for . . .*
11. It didn't enter his mind to call for help.   *No. He considered . . .*
12. The young man didn't consider giving him money.   *No. He insisted on . . .*
13. The young man didn't appreciate the ride.   *No. He thanked him for . . .*
14. John didn't want to get home.   *No. He looked forward to . . .*

II. John was naturally astonished by his strange experience. Take the parts of John and his wife, Martha, as he tells her about his exciting ride home.

GRAMMAR SUMMARY

GERUND CONSTRUCTIONS

A gerund is the *-ing* form of a verb when used as a noun. It is sometimes called a verbal noun*.

Examples: I like singing.
He gave up smoking last year.

*For spelling rules, see Chapter 2, page 13.

The following are *some* of the many verbs and expressions that are followed by a gerund:

Verbs: Stop, finish, quit, start, begin, like, love, enjoy, hate, detest, dislike, avoid, miss, deny, remember, admit, consider

Two-word verbs and verb + preposition combinations: give up, keep on, look forward to, put off, apologize for, think of, insist on, feel like, accuse (someone) of, arrest (someone) for, prevent (someone) from, thank (someone) for

Expressions: can't help, can't stand, what's the use of, have trouble/difficulty (in).

Examples:

John	detests	working for the telephone company.
	hates	
	dislikes	
	enjoys	
	loves	
	likes	

My uncle	gave up	smoking last month.
	quit	
	stopped	
	began	
	started	

He *finished* drinking his coffee and left the house.
Martha should try to *avoid* talking so long on the phone.
I *miss* talking to my brother.
I *remember* seeing her last week as I was getting off the bus.
He *denied* going to the bank last week.
If the children *keep on* arguing, I'll have to punish them.
I'm *looking forward to* going to Hong Kong.
I'm *thinking of* buying a car next month.
She *insisted on* driving me home.
He was *accused of* robbing a bank in St. Louis.
She was *arrested for* stealing the necklace.
He looked so funny, I *couldn't help* laughing.
What's the use of crying about it?
I've always had *trouble*   losing weight.
          difficulty (in)
They *admitted* taking the document.
We *considered* going early, but we changed our minds.
I *can't stand* getting up so early.

INTENSIVE PRACTICE

I. Expand the following cues by providing the appropriate verb.

Example: He likes _____ to the movies on Sundays.
He likes going to the movies on Sundays.

  1. They enjoy _____ a cocktail before dinner.
  2. We like _____ late on Sunday mornings.
  3. They can't stand _____ to pop music.
  4. I love _____ fresh milk for breakfast.
  5. Marvin hates _____ to strangers.
  6. We dislike _____ in such a polluted city.
  7. Anne enjoys _____ long letters.
  8. I don't enjoy _____ a bath in cold water.
  9. She dislikes _____ by plane.
 10. He hates _____ at the phone company.

II. Make sentences with *I'm thinking of*, and *but I'm not sure.* Use the cues provided.

Example: the beach this weekend
I'm thinking of going to the beach this weekend, but I'm not sure yet.

  1. a new car
  2. a cocktail party
  3. my boss for a raise
  4. a poem for my girlfriend
  5. New York next year

III. Combine the following sentences using the verb in parentheses and *when.*

Example: She screamed. She saw a face at the window.   (*start*)
She started screaming when she saw a face at the window.

  1. He smoked a lot. He got bronchitis.   (*quit*)
  2. She cried. Her mother came into the room.   (*stop*)
  3. He gambled a lot. He got married.   (*give up*)
  4. They had eaten. We came in.   (*finish*)
  5. Jane played tennis. She lost the championship.   (*give up*)
  6. He saw Betty every weekend. He met Helen.   (*stop*)
  7. He drank too much. His son died.   (*start*)
  8. She tried to be a model. They told her she was too   (*give up*)
     short.
  9. They laughed. I told them that joke.   (*begin*)
 10. She had painted the house. Her husband came home.   (*finish*)

IV. Use the cue in parentheses to make a sentence with *accused of* and/or *arrested for.* Begin your sentence with *My brother . . .*

Example: a bank (*rob*)
My brother was *accused of* (*arrested for*) robbing a bank.

1. a jewelry store   (*break into*)
2. diamonds across the border (*smuggle*)
3. a friend of his (*shoot*)
4. a car (*steal*)
5. his boss (*murder*)

V. Make sentences using *look forward to* and *enjoy*.

Example: to Miami (*go*)   travel

I'm looking forward to going to Miami. I've always enjoyed traveling.

look forward to	*enjoy*
1. the beach this weekend (*go*)	swim
2. my German course (*start*)	speak foreign languages
3. your parents (*meet*)	talk to nice people
4. to the casino (*go*)	gamble
5. that film (*see*)	watch good comedies

VI. Change the following quotes into gerund constructions using the cues on the right and the simple past tense.

Example: "I'd love to have some chocolate cake."   *He/feel like*
He felt like having some chocolate cake.

1. "I can't wait to go to Santiago."   *She/look forward to*
2. "I'm sorry I came late."   *He/apologize for*
3. "I'll buy the present tomorrow."   *He/put off*
4. "I didn't break the lamp."   *She/deny*
5. "We think of the accident all the   *We/can't help*
   time."
6. "I won't tell him the bad news   *She/avoid*
   until Thursday."
7. "We woke up several times last   *They/keep on*
   night."
8. "It was a difficult decision to   *Jack/have trouble*
   make."
9. "Let me drive you to the air-   *Laura/insist on*
   port."
10. "We used to eat out every Satur-   *Tom and Mary/miss*
    day night."
11. "I may sell my house to the   *He/think of*
    Smiths."
12. "I just couldn't put my shoes on."   *She/have difficulty in*
13. "You sent a present. Thank you."   *He/thank for*
14. "I think I'll buy a new car.   *He/consider*
15. "We stole the car."   *They/admit*

VII. Complete the following sentences with *what's the use of* and any appropriate comment.

Example: The exam will be in ten minutes, so *what's the use of studying now?*

1. Nobody will believe you, so _____ ?
2. The car's too old to be fixed, so _____ ?

3. The man is already dead, so _____ ?
4. We already have two radios, so _____ ?
5. You don't have any money in your account, so _____ ?

WRITING AND HOMEWORK

I. Fill in the blanks with an appropriate verb in the gerund form.

1. She apologized for _____, but her friends wouldn't forgive her.
2. I've always had trouble _____.
3. It's such a great day! I certainly don't feel like _____.
4. I tried to control myself, but I just couldn't help _____.
5. Let me know when your brother gets here. I'm looking forward to _____.
6. He put off _____ for so long that now he's in the hospital.
7. I told him I was feeling fine, but he insisted on _____.
8. Seatbelts in cars prevent a lot of people from _____.
9. Although the police questioned him for two days, he denied _____.
10. I shouted at her to stop, but she kept on _____.
11. He thanked me for _____. Nobody else remembered his birthday.
12. He admitted _____, when I asked him about the $2,000 phone bill.

II. Read the following short story.

The morning sun was coming through the small window, and Michael Mebs could feel its warmth on his skin. I'd give anything to be able to take a walk in the woods today, he thought to himself (*feel like*). A walk in the fresh air had always made him feel good (*enjoy*). He picked up his cup of coffee and put it mechanically to his lips (*start*). A few years ago, he and Marsha had planned to buy a country house in Maine (*think of*). He remembered how he had hesitated when they told him he would have to make a final decision (*put off*), secretly afraid to leave the comforts of the city. He drank the rest of his coffee (*finish*), and continued to dream in the warm sunshine (*keep on*). He tried not to think of Marsha but his thoughts went back to her constantly (*can't help*). He wanted to hear her voice (*miss*). He remembered how they used to go for long drives in the country every weekend (*love*).

The door opened and man in a dark gray suit came in. "Sorry I'm late," he said (*apologize for*). Hanson was his name. "Those reporters! I didn't talk to them (*avoid*). Why cooperate with people like that?" (*what's the use of*), he said angrily. "All they care about is getting a story."

"They're not going to believe me," said Mebs to his lawyer. "Don't give up now, Mike," said Hanson cheerfully, although he was very worried. He had never seen his client so depressed (*can't remember*). "I know how it will be," said Mebs slowly. He was finding it difficult to organize his thoughts (*have trouble*). "They will say I took the money (*accuse*), and I will tell them I don't know anything about the robbery (*deny*). But I want to tell you I'm grateful for all your help (*thank . . . for*)."

Rewrite the story, using the verbs in parentheses and an appropriate gerund. You will have to make a lot of changes in the text, but try to maintain the original idea of the story.

Example: (Refer to the text)

The morning sun was coming through the small window, and Michael Mebs could feel its warmth on his skin. I really feel like taking a walk in the woods today, he thought to himself (*or:* He felt like taking a walk in the woods). He had always enjoyed walking in the fresh air. He picked up his cup of coffee and started drinking (*or:* He started drinking his coffee) . . .

Now, continue the story.

III. Below you will find adjectives describing each sign of the zodiac. Choose one or more of the signs and write a description of the personality-type born under this sign. Use the following verbs, when possible: *like, love, enjoy, dislike, hate, look forward to, have trouble, can't help, insist on, avoid.*

Example: **Capricorn**—Dec. 22 to Jan. 19
            solitary, persistent, conservative, ambitious

Capricorns are solitary people. They like being alone and avoid going to parties and meeting people. Because they are persistent, they insist on finishing every job they start. Capricorns are conservative so they often have trouble adapting to changes and understanding new ideas. Capricorns avoid calling attention to themselves. Their ambition makes them hard workers, and they are usually successful in business.

Aquarius   Jan. 20 to Feb. 19
            creative, active, shy, unpunctual
Pisces   Feb. 19 to March 21
            romantic, sympathetic, complaining, unscientific
Aries   March 21 to April 20
            active, adventurous, impulsive, domineering, theatrical
Taurus   April 21 to May 20
            patient, stubborn, generous, musical, money-loving
Gemini   May 21 to June 21
            observant, talkative, cultured, impatient
Cancer   June 22 to July 22
            shy, evasive, easily hurt, domestic, conservative
Leo   July 23 to August 23
            arrogant, self-confident, pompous, honest, dramatic
Virgo   August 24 to September 23
            analytical, scientific, critical, efficient, literary

Libra	September 24 to October 23
	moderate, just, indecisive, pacifistic, artistic
Scorpio	October 24 to November 22
	energetic, determined, intelligent, passionate, vengeful
Sagittarius	November 23 to December 21
	freedom-loving, restless, optimistic, sociable, frank

DISCUSSION

1. Discuss the characteristics of the different signs of the zodiac with your classmates. How accurate is the description of your sign?
2. Numerology and astrology are both considered to be occult sciences: sciences that have been practiced for hundreds of years but that cannot be proved by modern scientific techniques. Do you believe that astrology and numerology are valid, or are they just nonsense? What about palmistry and card-reading?
3. What are some of the occult practices found in your country? Who practices them? Where are they practiced?
4. Do you believe that picking up hitchhikers is dangerous? Why? Why not?
5. Have you ever been a hitchhiker, or picked one up? Tell about your experiences.

BITS AND PIECES

Would you mind (not) . . . -ing

You are in the movie theater watching an Agatha Christie mystery you have waited a long time to see. Unfortunately, an obnoxious couple sitting right in front of you starts doing things that irritate and distract you:

1. She starts combing her hair
2. He starts smoking
3. She stands up to straighten her skirt
4. He starts eating popcorn noisily
5. She starts singing along with the background music
6. He starts telling the plot to the man next to him
7. She noisily starts looking through her handbag
8. She gets excited and starts jumping up and down in her seat
9. She starts calling to a friend in the front row
10. He drops something and starts looking under the seat for it
11. She puts on an enormous hat

12. He puts his feet up on the seat in front of him
13. He falls asleep and starts snoring

At first you try to be very polite, then you get impatient and start giving them orders.

I. Using the cues above, form a polite request, and then an impolite order in the affirmative.

Examples: She starts combing her hair
Would you mind putting your hands down, please. (polite)
Put your hands down! (impolite)

He starts smoking
Would you mind smoking somewhere else, please. (polite)
Put out that cigarette! (impolite)

II. Use the cues this time to form polite requests and impolite commands in the negative.

Examples: She starts combing her hair
Would you mind not combing your hair, please. (polite)
Don't come your hair like that! (impolite)

He starts smoking
Would you mind not smoking here, please. (polite)
Don't blow smoke in my direction! (impolite)

9

PRESENTATION

THINK FAST

I'd probably panic if our plane had engine trouble

The instructors at the School for Flight Attendants and Chef Le Pierre's School for Waiters are asking the students what they would do if certain unexpected situations occurred.

Take the parts of the instructors and the students. Ask and answer questions using the cues on the blackboards.

PICTURE A

Example: INSTRUCTOR: What would you do if a hijacker tried to take the plane to a different destination?

STUDENT: I would follow his instructions and try to keep the passengers calm. What's the use of trying to be a hero?

PICTURE B

Example: INSTRUCTOR: What would you do if a customer found a fly in his soup?

STUDENT: I would apologize and tell him that it had never happened before. Then I would bring him a new plate of soup and not put it on the bill.

EXPANSION

Read the following play, taking the parts of the characters: Peggy, Eleanor, Nancy, Pat, Terry, Jack, Greg, and Barry

The Reunion

ELEANOR: What's wrong with you tonight, Peggy? You don't look like you're having a good time. Don't you think this class reunion is fun?

PEGGY: I don't know . . . I just feel . . . I mean. Oh, what's the use of keeping it to myself!

BARRY: Come on, Peggy. You know you'd feel better if you told us.

PEGGY: OK. Let me ask you this. If you didn't have much money and you wanted to impress a rich man, would you tell him that you had a great job and lots of money?

NANCY: No, because if I did, he would find out sooner or later.

PEGGY: If you lived in a small apartment in the poor part of town, would you tell him you lived in a mansion?

GREG: If a girl told me lies like that, I'd never believe her again.

PEGGY: Well, do you remember Jack Torrence who went to Australia to make his fortune? I've been writing to him for three years and . . .

TERRY: Don't tell me you've been lying to him all this time in your letters!

PEGGY: Well, I suppose I *have* been exaggerating a little. And now this millionaire is going to walk through the door any minute, and I don't know what to do.

PAT: Well, if I were you, I'd keep on lying until I thought he was ready to accept the truth.

BARRY: That's no solution. If I were Peggy, I'd tell him right away.

NANCY: If he were *my* boyfriend and thought *I* had a lot of money, I'd rent a luxury apartment for a few days, and hope we left for Australia before my money ran out.

GREG: And what would you do if you ran out of money before you left for Australia?

NANCY: I'd borrow some more.

ELEANOR: But if he discovered the truth, he would probably never speak to you again.

TERRY: If I were you, I'd just forget about marrying him, Peggy.

PAT: Oh, look! Here comes Jack now! Doesn't he look great—like a million bucks!

GREG: Oh shut up, Pat. Well, go over and talk to him, Peggy—and tell him the truth.

(Peggy goes over to greet Jack)

JACK: You look wonderful, Peggy. It's so good to see you after all this time.

PEGGY: Jack, I have something to tell you . . .

JACK: Wait, Peggy. Let me ask you this first, before you say anything.

Would you still love me if I told you I'd lied about all the money I'd made in Australia?

PEGGY: (*smiles with relief*) Well, Jack, let's sit down. Something tells me we have a lot to talk about.

I. After practicing the parts, act out the play in the classroom. Try to memorize your lines.

II. Imagine that Jack is talking to his friends in Australia about his problem. Take the parts of Jack and his friends as they try to find a solution.

GRAMMAR SUMMARY

PAST CLAUSE + CONDITIONAL CLAUSE

The Second Conditional

The verb in the *if* clause is in the *simple past tense.* The verb in the main clause is in the *conditional, would + verb.*

AFFIRMATIVE

If I	had time, I	would travel more.
you	you	
she	she	
he	he	
we	we	
they	they	

We would buy a house if we were rich.

INTERROGATIVE

Would I quit working if I won the lottery?
Where would you go if you had the money?
What would he do if he were in your place?

NEGATIVE

I wouldn't go if I didn't have the money.
They wouldn't tell him that if they weren't sure.

I. The second conditional is used when the speaker wishes to hypothesize about a cause/effect situation that does not exist. The *if* clause (in the simple past tense) triggers the action in the *would* clause. Both clauses convey the idea of unreality and speculation.

Example: If I had enough money, I'd buy a new car.
(cause/simple past tense)   (effect/*would*)

I wouldn't talk to her if I were you.
(effect/*would*)   (cause/simple past tense)

    II. Either clause may come first.

Example: If I had time, I would get the tickets.
I would get the tickets if I had time.

    III. The verb *be* poses a special problem when used in the conditional. Although a great many speakers of American and British English use the standard conjugation of the verb *be* in the conditional, it is considered more appropriate to use *were* for all persons.

Example: If I (you, etc.) were younger, I'd (you'd, etc.) get married again.

    IV. The contracted form of *would* is almost always used in conversation and informal writing.

Example: I'd/he'd/she'd, etc., be happier if the exam were next week.

Notes

    i. *Should* for the first person singular and plural, though used in British English, is never used in conversational American English in conditional sentences.

Example: American English: If I were you, I would (*not* should) call him immediately.

    ii. Though some people prefer the use of subject pronouns after such phrases as: *If I were* (*he*), *if you were* (*she*), *if we were* (*they*), most native speakers use object pronouns.

Examples: If I were him, I'd leave town.

What would you do if you were her?

INTENSIVE PRACTICE

    I. Make statements beginning *If I were you . . .* using the following cues.

Example: so much noise   *If I were you, I wouldn't make so much noise.*

    1. the police
    2. that car
    3. so much money
    4. that French course
    5. his advice

    6. that medicine
    7. my job
    8. that movie
    9. that letter
    10. a vacation

    II. Ask questions with *Would you* _____ if _____ ? for the following statements.

Example: Laurie went to a party, even though she didn't like the hostess.
Would you go to a party if you didn't like the hostess?

1. He invited a girl to dinner, even though he didn't know her name.
2. She married a rich man, even though she didn't love him.
3. He ordered a large meal, even though he didn't have any money.
4. I wore that ugly shirt, even though I didn't like it.
5. He drove a car, even though he didn't have a license.

III. Complete the following sentences. Depending on the cues given, each clause may be either negative or affirmative.

Examples: A poor man says: If _____ a lot of money, I _____ around the world.
    If I had a lot of money, I'd travel around the world.

A light sleeper says: If I _____ in such a noisy neighborhood, I _____ better at night.
    If I didn't live in such a noisy neighborhood, I'd sleep better at night.

1. A fat man says: If _____ so much, I _____ so fat.
2. A busy woman says: If _____ more time, I _____ the movies.
3. A bad student says: If _____ more, I _____ better grades.
4. An ugly girl says: If _____ prettier, I _____ as a model.
5. A tired woman says: If _____ more rest, I _____ better.
6. A chain smoker says: If _____ so much, I _____ such a bad cough.
7. A short man says: If _____ so short, I _____ basketball.
8. A lonely man says: If _____ a girlfriend, I _____ so lonely.
9. A fat man says: If _____ more exercise, I _____ so fat.
10. A coffee drinker says: If _____ so much coffee, I _____ trouble sleeping.

IV. Change the following sentences so that they begin with an *if* clause. Depending on the sentence, the clause may be either affirmative or negative.

Examples: She isn't in love with him, so she won't marry him.
    If she were in love with him, she would marry him.

    I hate liver, so I don't eat it.
    If I didn't hate liver, I would eat it.

1. He doesn't know the answer, so he can't tell you.
2. He spends a lot of money, so he doesn't have money at the end of the month.

3. They are rich, so they buy a new car every year.
4. He has a cold, so he isn't going to play basketball tonight.
5. I need money, so I'm looking for a job.
6. She eats a lot, so she keeps on getting fatter.
7. Janice doesn't like bananas, so she doesn't eat them.
8. He doesn't go to class often, so he gets bad grades.
9. They don't have time, so they don't write often.
10. They study a lot, so they're always tired.
11. Jim wears glasses, so he can see better than I can.
12. Marge isn't old enough, so they won't let her into the theater.

V. Make questions for the following answers. Begin with *What would he/she/you do if. . . ?*

Examples: I'd call the police immediately.
What would you do if someone broke into your home?

She'd punish him and send him to bed early.
What would she do if she saw her son playing with matches?

1. I'd tell him that smoking in elevators was not allowed.
2. I'd exchange it for another dress.
3. She'd divorce him.
4. He'd go on a diet.
5. I'd call the fire department.
6. He'd wait for the next train.
7. I'd take him to the hospital.
8. She'd take his exam paper away and fail him.
9. I'd have another set of keys made.
10. I'd buy an expensive car and a house in the country.

WRITING AND HOMEWORK

I. Fill in the blanks.

1. What _____ you do if someone _____ your car?
2. I _____ a house in the country if _____ a lot of money.
3. His mother _____ him if she _____ he had started smoking.
4. I _____ him the truth if I _____ you.
5. I _____ you to the airport if I _____ the time.
6. If she _____ so much, she _____ an ulcer.
7. If I _____ a crime, I _____ the police right away.
8. If you _____ rich, where _____ live?
9. If he _____ honest, I _____ him some money.
10. Where _____ you go if _____ anywhere in the world?

II. First Aid Quiz

Many people would not know what to do in an emergency. Would you? Choose the correct answer for each of the four items below and justify your choice. Explain what you think would happen if you chose one of the other three possibilities.

1. If a friend of yours got an electric shock, would you . . .
   a. try to pull him away from the source of the shock?
   b. throw water on him?
   c. turn off the electricity at the source?
   d. pull him away using a metal bar?
2. What would you do if a friend of yours cut his arm badly with a knife?
   a. massage the arm to improve circulation.
   b. put pressure on the wound using a clean bandage.
   c. put the wound under hot water to clean it.
   d. distract the victim by keeping him active.
3. If you found a person unconscious, would you . . .
   a. give him a glass of water to drink?
   b. lightly massage his body with alcohol?
   c. slap the victim's face until he regained consciousness?
   d. put the victim on his stomach with his head turned to the side?
4. If a person burned himself severely, would you . . .
   a. cover the burns with bandages and keep the patient warm?
   b. try to clean the burned area with very cold water?
   c. break the blisters and make sure the victim was cool?
   d. move the patient to a cool place and wash the burns with alcohol?

III. Many people write to Linda Lovelorn asking for personal advice on different matters. Answer the following letters for Linda, using *If I were you . . .* whenever possible.

1. I am in love with a man who is twenty years older than me and want to marry him. What should I do?
2. A good friend of mine has asked me to help him during a final exam. It's dangerous, but I am afraid to say "no." What should I do?
3. I do not like the young man my daughter intends to marry.
4. My husband's mother constantly criticizes me. I want to tell her off, but I'm afraid of hurting my husband.
5. My son is a senior in high school. He says he is tired of studying and wants to get a job. What should I tell him? I don't want him to quit school.
6. I'm a university student and I have the impression that my history professor doesn't like me. I work very hard and really want to pass this course. What should I do?
7. My boss has given everyone in the company a raise but me. I don't know why. I am shy, and my boss is a difficult person to talk to. What should I do?

8. I am divorced and have a ten-year-old daughter. I intend to marry again, and my fiancé and I love each other deeply. My daughter hates him, though.

9. My husband pays more attention to his TV football games than to me. He doesn't know I exist when a football game is on.

10. I am a widow with five children. I am in love with a divorced man who has six children. Is marriage the right thing for us?

DISCUSSION

I. What would you do if you were in these situations? Read the quotes and discuss each one.

1. "We were going up in the elevator. There were six of us inside, and we had just reached the seventh floor when there was a terrible sound of something breaking. Then the elevator stopped and the lights went off."

KATHY SHEA, journalist

2. "It was 2:00 in the morning. I was driving along a lonely, country road and there wasn't another car in sight. The next thing I knew, my car was out of gas."

WILLIAM TAORMINA, taxi driver

3. "I was sitting in the train station when a stranger came up to me and shoved an overnight bag into my hand and said, 'Watch this for me, will you?' When he didn't come back after an hour, I started to worry about what I was holding."

RAFAEL FUENTES, engineer

4. "You can imagine how I felt when on my first day of teaching, a student fell asleep in my class."

BOB CROFT, teacher

5. "I was hearing confession when the unexpected happened. 'I've committed two murders,' said one of my parishioners, 'and I'm going to commit another one tonight, Father.' He sounded very determined, but I had to keep his secret."

FATHER ROY HARRIS, priest

II. 1. Discuss the results of the First Aid Quiz in the *Writing and Homework* section with your classmates.

2. Reverse the theme of *The Reunion*. Instead of two poor young people, two very rich people have told each other in letters that they are poor because they don't want to be loved only for their money. Take the roles of the different characters and re-enact the play.

BITS AND PIECES

You had better (not) . . .

Had better (not) is used to express strong advice or warning.

I. Mrs. Harris, the worried mother in Chapter 7, is giving her son some strong advice about what to do to prepare for his trip to Europe. Complete the sentences, using *you'd better*.

Example: You never know when it will rain, so _____.
You never know when it will rain, so you'd better take an umbrella with you.

1. The flights usually fill up fast in August, so _____.
2. You might get airsick on the plane, so _____.
3. Summer nights are cool in England, so _____.
4. It's dangerous to carry cash around, so _____.
5. If you get a hotel outside of town, you'll spend too much time traveling, so _____.
6. You will want to know a few French phrases before you go, so _____.
7. You may not find that medicine in Europe, so _____.
8. You'll want to take pictures of all the places you visit, so _____.
9. Your feet will hurt after all the sight-seeing, so _____.
10. It's easy to get lost in Munich, so _____.

II. Children are always getting into trouble, as you saw in Chapter 7. Referring to the picture on page 59, imagine what the mother of these children would say if she came into the room and caught them. Use *You'd better not,* and add the probable consequence.

Example: You'd better not lean out the window, or you'll fall.

PRESENTATION

PEOPLE AND PASTIMES

I've been playing the guitar since I was sixteen years old.

The following people were interviewed by David Snow on his TV talk show *Faces in Focus.*

I. Take the parts of David Snow and each of the above characters. Reconstruct the interviews using the cues provided. Use the following example as a model:

Example:

DAVID SNOW: How long have you been president of Apex Inc., Mr. Segovia?
SAM SEGOVIA: Well David, I've been president of this company for five years.
DAVID SNOW: I hear you're an excellent guitarist!
SAM SEGOVIA: Well, I've certainly had enough practice. I've been playing the guitar since I was sixteen years old.

II. Using the cues beside each picture, ask and answer questions about the characters.

Example: How long has Sam Segovia been president of Apex Inc.?
He's been president of Apex Inc. for five years.
How long has he been playing the guitar?
He's been playing the guitar since he was sixteen years old.

III. Extend each interview to include more questions and answers.

EXPANSION

Read the following short play taking the parts of the headwaiter, Harry, Myrtle, man, woman, waiter.

Myrtle Meets a Movie Star

HEADWAITER: How many in your party, sir?

HARRY: Just my wife and myself.

MYRTLE: Yes. We'd like a table for two—in the middle of the restaurant so we can see everyone who comes in. You see, I've been dying to come to Hollywood ever since I was a young girl. I've heard a lot of stars come here—

HARRY: Myrtle, I'm sure this gentleman is not interested in your life story.

MYRTLE: —and today is our wedding anniversary—we've been married for thirty years. Isn't that just wonderful?

HEADWAITER: That's simply fascinating, Madam. This is your table, sir. Have a nice meal.

WAITER: Would you like to order now? I recommend the pepper steak, it's—

MYRTLE: Waiter, I suppose you've seen thousands of movie stars. How long have you been working here?

WAITER: I've been working here for twenty-five years, and I've seen all the greats—Gable, Cooper, Monroe, Wayne, Newman—I've been serving stars ever since I was a young man.

MYRTLE: How long have you been living in Hollywood?

HARRY: We'll have the pepper steak, please.

FOUR HOURS LATER

HARRY: Myrtle, you must admit I've been patient this time. We've been sitting here for four hours and not one star has come in.

MYRTLE: Just drink your coffee, Harry. I'm not leaving until I see a movie star!

HARRY: But I've been drinking coffee for three hours . . .

MYRTLE: Harry! I don't believe it! Robert Redford and his wife are coming this way! I've been waiting for this moment for years! (*she gets up*) Oh, Mr. Redford! This is wonderful! I've been a fan of yours ever since I saw you in *Butch Cassidy.*

MAN: I'm not Robert Redford, ma'am. Scrubb's the name. Huey Scrubb.

MYRTLE: I know you're Robert Redford. I've seen all your movies! My daughter has had a picture of you on her wall for years! You're Robert Redford!

WOMAN: I beg your pardon but I've been married to this man for fifteen years, and I can assure you he's Huey Scrubb. Will you excuse us? We've been walking around all day, and we'd like something to eat.

MYRTLE: (*raising her voice*) You're Robert Redford! *Please* give me your autograph.

MAN: Huey Scrubb's my name!

WOMAN: Waiter! This woman's been bothering us! She says my husband is Robert Redford. Could you please tell her to stop annoying us?

HEADWAITER: We've had Robert Redford in here hundreds of times, and this is not him!

HARRY: I've been patient with you, Myrtle, but this time you've gone too far!

MYRTLE: I've been waiting for a chance like this for years . . . and now he won't give me his autograph.

WAITER: (*to man*) Give her your autograph. Maybe this way she'll leave you alone.

MAN: OK (*writes*) "To my favorite fan, from Robert Redford" (*gives piece of paper to Myrtle*)

MYRTLE: Thanks. Hey, wait! This is not Robert Redford's signature. Of all the nerve! You're an imposter! How long have you been going around telling people you're Robert Redford?

HARRY: Let's go, Myrtle. I've been patient long enough. We're leaving. (*they go*)

HEADWAITER: I've been working here for thirty years, and I've had all kinds of trouble with customers, but never like this!

WAITER: It's that poor guy I feel sorry for. He's had the *same* trouble for thirty years.

Set up a restaurant scene in the classroom with chairs, tables, and any other props you can find. Re-enact the play *Myrtle Meets a Movie Star* using dialogue from the play when you can remember it and your own words when you cannot. Try not to refer to the play. Use the cues below:

HEADWAITER: asks how many people are in their party
HARRY: responds
MYRTLE: tells where she wants to sit and tells about her desire to come to Hollywood
HARRY: tries to keep Myrtle quiet
MYRTLE: tells the headwaiter about their anniversary
HEADWAITER: shows polite but bored interest and shows them to their table
WAITER: tries to take their order
MYRTLE: asks about the waiter's experience with movie stars

WAITER: answers Myrtle's question
MYRTLE: asks about waiter's residence in Hollywood
HARRY: (*interrupting*) orders their meal

FOUR HOURS LATER

HARRY: shows impatience and talks about how long they've been there
MYRTLE: tells Harry to drink his coffee and expresses desire to stay
HARRY: complains about all the coffee he's drunk
MYRTLE: expresses astonishment at seeing Robert Redford; approaches him and praises him
MAN: tells his real name
MYRTLE: tells why she *knows* he's Robert Redford
WOMAN: tells why she knows he's *not* Robert Redford
MYRTLE: insists; asks for autograph
WOMAN: calls waiter and complains
HEADWAITER: tells why he knows man is not Robert Redford
WAITER: suggests that the man give her his autograph
MAN: writes personal autograph for Myrtle
MYRTLE: accuses man of being an imposter
HARRY: takes Myrtle away
HEADWAITER: talks about his thirty years of problems
WAITER: talks about Harry's thirty-year problem

GRAMMAR SUMMARY

THE PRESENT PERFECT TENSE

Questions with How long? *Responses with* for *and* since.

    I. **The Present Perfect Continuous:** *have/has + been + -ing* form of verb.

Questions with *How long?* + the present perfect continuous, and statements with the present perfect continuous + *for* or *since,* indicate a long or extended action that continues into the present. Most verbs in English can be used in the continuous form.

Example: How long have you been studying English?
        I've been studying it | for two years.
                      | since 1982.

    II. **The Present Perfect:** *have/has* + past participle of verb.

Certain verbs in English cannot be used in the continuous form even though they are used for long or extended actions. Four of the most common are: *be, have* (possession), *know,* and *like.*

Examples: How long have you been a doctor?
         I've been a doctor | for ten years.
                   | since 1974.

How long have you had a car?
I've had one |for five years.
          |since 1979.

How long have you known him?
I've known him |for six months.
            |since January.

How long have you liked jazz?
I've liked |it for years.
         |since I was a kid.

III. Usage

    A. Questions with *How long* and the present perfect indicate a period of time that began in the past and continues into the present.

Examples: How long have they been living in New York? (They are still living in New York.)

How long has he been an architect? (He is still an architect.)

    B. Statements with *for* + a period of time (two years, three days, six weeks, etc.) indicate that an action began in the past and continues into the present. The *duration* of time is emphasized with *for*.

Examples: They've been waiting for two hours. (They began waiting two hours ago and are still waiting.)

I've had my car for three years. (I bought it three years ago, and I still have it.)

    C. Statements with *since* + a point of time or an event in the past (last January, 1975, Wednesday, the Second World War, yesterday morning, etc.) indicate that an action began at the stated time or upon the stated occasion and continues into the present. Here the *starting point* of the action is emphasized rather than the duration.

Examples: He's been wearing those socks since Friday. (And he is still wearing them.)

We've lived in Atlanta since my sister was born. (And we still live there.)

Notes

i. *Work* and *live* are two verbs that are used with *How long?, for,* and *since* in both the continuous and simple forms of the present perfect.

Example: How long have you |been working |in California?
                                |worked |

I've |been working |there for four years.
   |worked |

ii. *All* + a time period, e.g. *all day, all my life,* is often used with the present to indicate an extended action continuing into the present. As with *for,* the duration of time is emphasized.

Example: I've been working hard all day.

iii. The contracted form of *have/has* is usually employed in speaking and informal writing.

Example: I've (He's) been looking for an apartment since October.

iv. *Long* is frequently used to replace *for a long time* in interrogative and negative sentences.

Examples: Have you been waiting long?
I haven't been working here long.

INTENSIVE PRACTICE

I. Supply affirmative responses for the following questions using the cues in parentheses. Depending on the cue, use *for, since,* or *all* + a time period.

Examples: Is she still typing those letters?   *(two hours)*
Yes. She's been typing them *for two hours.*

Is it raining?   *(one o'clock)*
Yes. It's been raining *since one o'clock.*

Is he still trying to call New York?   *(all morning)*
Yes. He's been trying *all morning.*

1. Is he really the president of Apex Inc.?   *(1976)*
2. Are you feeling sick?   *(all week)*
3. Is Paul still studying?   *(one o'clock)*
4. Is he still wearing that same shirt?   *(two days)*
5. Are the children still sleeping?   *(four o'clock)*
6. Are they still arguing?   *(all evening)*
7. Are they married?   *(several years)*
8. Is he still waiting for that phone call?   *(two o'clock this afternoon)*
9. Is that woman still talking on the phone?   *(an hour and a half)*
10. Is your brother still working on his car?   *(two days)*

II. Complete the following using the present perfect, an appropriate verb, and either *for* or *since.*

Examples: He _____ TV _____ an hour.
He's been watching TV for an hour.

She _____ for the bus _____ two o'clock.
She's been waiting for the bus since two o'clock.

1. Denise _____ in Boston _____ 1967.
2. They _____ for the Ford Motor Company _____ seven years.

3. The secretary _____ those letters _____ an hour and a half.
4. We _____ swimming lessons _____ last summer.
5. They _____ in the doctor's office _____ two hours.
6. She _____ for her exams _____ last month.
7. Harry _____ on the phone _____ three o'clock.
8. He _____ cough medicine _____ a long time.
9. Janet _____ for the French test _____ a week.
10. She _____ basketball _____ eight o'clock.

III. Complete the following questions using *How long . . .* and a logical verb in the present perfect continuous tense.

Example: you/piano lessons?

How long have you been taking piano lessons?

1. you/your vacations in Miami?
2. they/out together?
3. Janis/in that apartment
4. he/*Shine* hair cream?
5. Bob/glasses?
6. he/in that factory?
7. they/love letters to each other?
8. you/your clothes in that department store?
9. you/concerts?
10. he/for his final exams?

IV. Complete the following using the present perfect. Use *know* in the first section, *have* in the second, and *be* in the third.

Examples: I _____ Margaret _____ children.
I've known Margaret since we were children.

Mary _____ that typewriter _____ 1978.
Mary has had that typewriter since 1978.

He _____ a doctor _____ 1960.
He's been a doctor since 1960.

Know

1. I _____ him all my life.

2. My husband _____ them _____ twenty-five years.

3. How long _____ Janis _____ your brother?

4. They _____ each other _____ 1965.

5. How long _____ you and Bob _____ each other?

Be

1. How long _____ he _____ in the hospital?

2. They _____ at home all day.

3. I _____ a student _____ four years.

4. She _____ in England _____ two weeks.

5. How long _____ Bob _____ an accountant?

Have

1. He _____ that car _____ ten years.
2. I _____ a headache _____ I got up.

3. They _____ that yacht _____ last year.
4. She _____ a sore throat all week.
5. I _____ these glasses _____ October.

V. Complete the following questions and answers. Use a logical verb + the present perfect tense in the question, and *ever since* + the simple past tense in the answer.

Example: How long _____ she _____ in Paris?
(her mother *die*)

How long has she been living in Paris?
She's been living in Paris ever since her mother died.

1. How long _____ Marsha _____ cooking lessons?
   (*get* married)
2. How long _____ he _____ glasses?
   (*be* a child)
3. How long _____ you _____ this brand of cigarettes?
   (*be* a teenager)
4. How long _____ Jack _____ on crutches?
   (*break* his leg)
5. How long _____ Mike _____ model planes?
   (*be* a young boy)
6. How long _____ he _____ jet planes?
   (*get* his pilot's license)
7. How long _____ they _____ on the island?
   (their ship *sink*)
8. How long _____ he _____ in love with Jane?
   (*meet* her)
9. How long _____ Bob and Joan _____ at their parents' house?
   (their own house *burn down*)
10. How long _____ you _____ sick?
    (*eat* that hamburger?)

VI. Ask questions beginning *Have you (Has he, she, it, etc.)*
    been _____ -ing?

Example: Have they been fighting long?
Yes. This is the fifteenth round, and nobody has been knocked out yet.

1. _____ long?
   Yes, since eight. I think I'll wake him up soon.
2. _____ long?
   Yes, for four days. It's the worst snow storm we've had in years.
3. _____ long?
   You'd better believe it! And I can't see a thing without them.
4. _____ long?
   Yes, since nine o'clock. It's about time you got here!
5. _____ long?
   Yes, for ten years. That's why my teeth are so yellow.

6. _____ long?
   Yes, all my life. I love this neighborhood.
7. _____ long?
   No, my first date with Jack was just last week.
8. _____ long?
   Yeah, for years—since the factory opened, in fact.
9. _____ long?
   No, our first lesson was last week.
10. _____ long?
   Yes, for the past two weeks. I suppose I should see a doctor.

WRITING AND HOMEWORK

I. Complete the following.

1. How long _____ they _____ for the bus?
2. _____ he _____ French lessons long?
3. He's a good friend of mine. I _____ him for ten years.
4. Phyllis _____ sick ever since she had dinner at that new restaurant.
5. How long _____ your brother _____ a psychiatrist?
6. Doctor! You have to help me! I _____ this stomach ache for three days.
7. _____ they _____ married long?
8. Nancy _____ on the phone all morning.
9. How long _____ she _____ as a secretary?
10. Those children _____ television all evening.

II. Write about the following inventions. Mention the name of the inventor and tell how long people or certain groups of people have been using each invention.

Example: People have been wearing nylon since the Du Pont laboratories invented it in 1937.

People have been wearing nylon for nearly fifty years, ever since the Du Pont laboratories invented it in 1937.

FAMOUS INVENTIONS

1. stethoscope	Laënnec	1819
2. piano	Cristofori	1709
3. aspirin	Dreser	1893
4. phonograph	Edison	1877
5. ballpoint pen	Loud	1888
6. margarine	Mège-Mouries	1869
7. bifocal lenses	Ben Franklin	1784
8. motorcycles	Daimler	1885
9. electric razor	Schick	1931
10. long playing records	Goldmark	1948

III. Pedro da Costa says, "I've been living in the U.S. for two years, and working at Jackson's Bookstore for three months. I've been studying English at night for two months now . . .

Write ten facts about yourself, using the present perfect continuous to refer to *where you live, your job, studies, hobbies, habits.*

DISCUSSION

I. The following people have special interests that are not related to their professional activities. Their names and professions are listed on the left, and their special interests on the right. Working in pairs, take the parts of a reporter and of one of the people listed. The reporter should try to find out as much information as possible.

Horace Dart, shoe salesman	fortune telling
Monica Chang, university student	Olympic swimmer
Sidney Shaft, doctor	mystery story writer
Greg Prentice, window washer	secret agent
Doris Shavinsky, tour guide	amateur archaeologist

II. The following movie stars are being interviewed by the press. One student should take the part of the star who will provide the answers. The rest of the class will be reporters asking for the information. The student playing the part of the movie star may want to use the information below to help him answer the questions.

Elizabeth Gaynor
1. Born—London 1932
2. First film—*The Girl with the Horse,* 1944
3. Other famous films—*The Queen of the Nile,* 1960; *Suddenly Last Winter,* 1958; *Who's Afraid of Oscar Wilde?,* 1967
4. Oscar—Best Actress, 1964
5. Husbands—Jimmie Tips (1949–1952); Freddie Fishman (1953–1958); Rod Mitchell (1958–1960); Richard Bard (1962–1968); Mike Aspen (1974–   )
6. Interests and hobbies—reading and painting
7. Residence in Hollywood—1962 to present
8. Children—Reginald, 1952; Janet, 1956; Louise, 1960

Michael Newbury
1. Born—1940
2. First film—*Buffalo,* 1958
3. Other famous films—*Mud* 1963; *The Cowboy Meets the Kid,* 1966; *The Duke,* 1968; *Running Wild,* 1978.
4. Married to—Wendy Storm
5. Interests and hobbies—automobile racing, 2nd prize Le Mans 1978; antique collection; film making
6. Residence in Hollywood—1967 to present
7. Children—Tina, 1963; Jason, 1966; David, 1970

BITS AND PIECES

Ever Since

The expression *ever since* is used when the speaker wants to emphasize the importance or duration of a time period or event.

Examples: I've liked Beethoven ever since I heard the Fifth Symphony.   (importance of the event emphasized)

I've been sitting here ever since you left.   (length of time emphasized)

Some Hollywood stars are talking about their careers. Use the information in quotes to make sentences with *ever since*. Remember to use the simple present perfect with the verbs *be, have,* and *like*. Use the present perfect continuous with the other verbs.

Examples: "When I become a star I decided that diamond bracelets were the only kind for me."
She's been wearing diamond bracelets ever since she became a star.

"I made *Moonlight and Roses.* It was an immediate success. Because of that movie I am now one of Hollywood's most famous actors."
He's been famous ever since he made the film Moonlight and Roses.

1. "I saw *Gone With the Wind.* Right then I decided that I wanted to make a historical film."
2. "I got to Hollywood and started looking for a job. I haven't found one yet."
3. "I started acting lessons as a child. I still take them for professional reasons.
4. "The director told me I had a terrible voice. That's why I'm taking voice lessons."
5. "I saw myself on the screen. I was so shocked that I decided to eat just one meal a day."
6. "A book about Charlie Chaplin is what got me interested in movies."
7. "I started singing as a child."
8. "I started making movies when Zanuck discovered me in 1947."
9. "Gene Kelly in *An American in Paris* was on TV. I got up and started dancing around the room. As you can see, I haven't stopped dancing yet."
10. "I'm not like most stars. Tom came back from the war, and we got married. We're still together."
11. "I made *The Monster at Midnight,* and it was such a success that now horror movies are the only ones I appear in."
12. "I jumped into the director's pool with all my clothes on. That was five weeks ago, and I still have a cold."
13. "The director told me I was too old to play the part. I haven't stopped crying since."

PRESENTATION

DARLING ROSEMARY AND DEAREST BILL

You rat! You've been lying to me!

Bill Rubin and Rosemary Gibbs have been engaged for three years. Bill is away at college, and Rosemary is the assistant manager of a small firm. In their letters, Bill and Rosemary have not been honest with each other about what they've been doing lately.

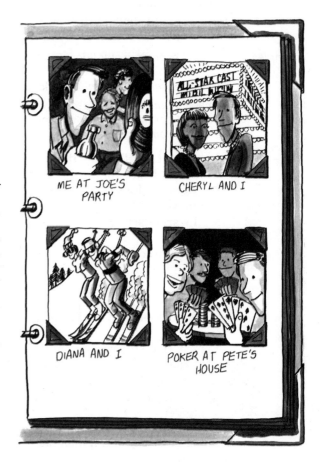

ME AT JOE'S PARTY

CHERYL AND I

DIANA AND I

POKER AT PETE'S HOUSE

My Darling Rosemary,

Sorry for not writing sooner, but I've been really busy lately. My final exams are coming up soon and I've been studying every night until two a.m.

Professor Smiley has been giving us a lot of work to do, so this means I've been spending most of my free time in the library and the biology lab.

You wouldn't recognize me: I've been living on cheese sandwiches and drinking black coffee to keep awake. I've lost ten pounds and I've been getting a lot of headaches and generally feeling terrible.

What have you been doing? Please write soon and cheer me up.

All my love,

Bill

My Dearest Bill,

I'm sorry I haven't had time to write before now, but that awful boss of mine, Mr. Snow, has been keeping me really busy. I've been working late almost every night, contacting important clients and writing reports.

In what used to be my spare time, I've been doing research for one of Mr. Snow's projects.

I hope you've been thinking of me as much as I've been thinking of you. Dying to hear from you.

Kisses and hugs,

Rosemary

I. Read the two letters and then look at the photo albums, which show what Bill and Rosemary have *really* been doing. Tell what they have really been doing during their separation.

II. Bill and Rosemary have just discovered the truth about each other. Re-enact their phone conversation.

Example: ROSEMARY: You rat! You haven't been studying every night. You've been going to parties and having a good time!

BILL: Look who's talking! You haven't been working late every night! You've been having dinner with your boss!

EXPANSION

I. Read the following short play, taking the parts of the characters.

Middleton's Mysterious Virus

MR. JACOBSON: I'd like to see the doctor, please. My name is Jacobson, Louis Jacobson.

RECEPTIONIST: Do you have an appointment, Mr. Jacobson?

MR. JACOBSON: At 4:30. Can you hurry? I'm in terrible pain. It's that mysterious virus that's been going around Middleton lately. I think I've got it.

RECEPTIONIST: You too? I'll see what I can do. Please have a seat.

(enter Mr. DiAngelo)

MR. JACOBSON: DiAngelo! This is a surprise! I haven't seen you for ages! What are you doing here?

MR. DIANGELO: Brother! I've been feeling really awful lately. It's these terrible stomach cramps I've been getting for about three weeks now. They say there's some strange virus—

MR. JACOBSON: What a coincidence! Me too! I've been suffering from stomach cramps since last month—and getting about two hours of sleep a night because of it, too!

(enter Mr. Carver)

MR. DIANGELO: Look! Here comes Fred Carver. Hey, Fred! What have you been doing with yourself lately?

MR. CARVER: I've been going crazy. *That's* what I've been doing. I think I might have an ulcer. I've been having these awful cramps for about three weeks. I've been taking all kinds of medicine for them too, but nothing has worked. If it's not an ulcer, then it's that virus that's been going around recently.

(enter Mrs. Simpson and Mrs. White)

Hey! Here comes Alice Simpson and Dora White. What's up, ladies?

MRS. WHITE: My whole family has been suffering from that virus that's been attacking Middleton. Maybe Dr. Mendes can figure it out. It's a mystery to me.

MR. SIMPSON: I've been feeling so terrible recently that I decided to see Dr. Mendes too. It must be some chemical they've been putting in the water. What else could it be?

MRS. WHITE: Have you been washing your fresh vegetables? *I* have. I figure you can never be sure. Cholera, you know.

MRS. SIMPSON: No! It's that strange virus. The Middleton virus.

RECEPTIONIST: The doctor will see you in a few minutes, Mr. Jacobson. Hello, Dora. Alice, you here too? You know I saw your husband at the cooking class last night. Chef Le Pierre has certainly been showing us some marvelous new recipes!

MRS. SIMPSON: I know. We've been eating a different dish every night; Henry really makes a marvelous gourmet meal. That Chef Le Pierre is certainly imaginative!

MR. JACOBSON: You say your husband's been taking classes at the cooking school with Chef Le Pierre, Mrs. Simpson? So has my wife. She's been going for about three weeks.

MR. DIANGELO: So has my wife.

MR. CARVER: And mine.

MRS. WHITE: And my husband!

(they all get up and go to the door)

RECEPTIONIST: Hey! Where are you all going? You all have appointments with Dr. Mendes!

MR. CARVER: Tell Dr. Mendes that I think we've discovered the terrible virus that's been attacking Middleton.

MR. JACOBSON: Yeah! Le Pierre-itis:

MRS. WHITE: If he doesn't find anything about it in the medical journals, tell him to consult a cookbook!

(they leave)

II. After discovering the cause of their illness, Mr. Jacobson, Mr. DiAngelo, Mr. Carver, Mrs. Simpson, and Mrs. White decide to have a talk with Chef Le Pierre. Take the parts of the six characters as they argue about the problem.

GRAMMAR SUMMARY

RECENTLY/LATELY

I. *Recently* and *lately* + the present perfect continuous indicate that an action began at some undefined time in the recent past and continues into the present.

Examples: I've been thinking about you recently.
Have you been thinking about me recently?
I haven't been thinking about you recently.

He's been taking a lot of medicine lately.
Has he been taking a lot of medicine lately?
He hasn't been taking a lot of medicine lately.

II. The present perfect continuous is often used without the words *recently* and *lately* to denote a recent action that began in the past and continues into the present. Although the actual words have been omitted, the idea of *recently* or *lately* is implied.

Examples: I've been feeling really sick.

What have you been doing?

I haven't been going to my classes.

III. In order to emphasize the number of times that a given action has been happening recently or lately, expressions like *almost every night, a lot, every day,* etc., are often used.

Examples: I've been working late almost every night.

Has the baby been crying a lot?

She's been studying every night until midnight.

IV. The verb *be* + an adjective is often used with or without the words *recently* or *lately* to indicate a recent past state that continues into the present.

Examples: I've been | busy | (recently, lately)
                         | ill |
                         | worried |
                         | cold |
                         | depressed |

INTENSIVE PRACTICE

I. Complete the following using *recently* or *lately* and the cues in parentheses.

Example: My husband _____ very hard.   (*work*)
My husband has been working very hard recently/lately.

1. Paul _____ golf with his boss a lot   (*play*)
2. I _____ a lot of headaches   (*get*)
3. You _____ too much   (*smoke*)
4. My mother _____ awful   (*feel*)
5. Terry _____ a lot of classes   (*miss*)
6. Judy _____ a lot of new clothes   (*buy*)
7. Our refrigerator _____ a lot   (*break down*)
8. I _____ a few piano lessons   (*give*)
9. The teacher _____ us a lot of homework   (*assign*)
10. Our car _____ a funny noise   (*make*)

II. Complete the following using the *negative* and the verbs in parentheses.

Example: Carol _____ well at all lately.   (*look*)
Carol hasn't been looking well at all lately.

1. Doctor, I _____ well lately.   (*feel*)
2. Tom _____ very hard recently.   (*work*)
3. The baby _____ very well lately.   (*sleep*)
4. This camera _____ very good pictures recently. (*take*)
5. Ben _____ much weight lately.   (*lose*)

III. Substitute the following in place of *you* in the model. Make all other necessary changes as well.

Model: What have *you* been doing lately? I haven't seen you in ages!

Example: Bill—What has *Bill* been doing lately? I haven't seen him in ages.

1. your sister   4. Melanie
2. Tom   5. the Wilsons
3. they   6. Louisa

7. your brother   9. Mr. Cummings
8. your parents   10. Bob and Martha

IV. Complete the following questions and answers. Use the verbs in parentheses for the answer.

Example: What _____ you _____ doing lately?
I _____ hard, as usual.   *(work)*
What have you been doing lately?
I've been working hard, as usual.

1. How _____ Mr. Watson _____ feeling lately?
   He _____ a lot better.   *(feel)*
2. How _____ Tom _____ getting along lately?
   Well, he _____ a lot of trouble with his job.   *(have)*
3. How _____ your classes _____ going lately?
   Well, our professor _____ us work hard.   *(make)*
4. What _____ Bob and Laurie _____ doing lately?
   Not much. They _____ home a lot.   *(stay)*
5. What _____ your sister _____ doing lately?
   She _____ to parties and _____ a good time.   *(go; have)*

V. Complete the first sentences below so that the second sentences make sense.

Example: *You've been eating too much.* That's why you have a stomach ache.

1. Florence _____. That's why her Spanish is improving.
2. He _____. That's why he has a black eye.
3. We _____. That's why our feet are so sore.
4. I _____. That's why I'm on a diet.
5. My brother _____. That's why his boss is angry with him.
6. I _____. That's why I'm so sunburned.
7. Harvey _____. That's why he looks so sick.
8. Roberta _____. That's why she's so broke.
9. It _____. That's why my umbrella's all wet.
10. She _____. That's why her eyes are so red.

WRITING AND HOMEWORK

I. Complete the following:

MR. SMITH: I (feel) _____ awful lately, Doctor.
DOCTOR: What seems to be your problem, Mr. Smith?
MR. SMITH: I (sleep, *negative*) _____ very much and I (gain)
_____ a lot of weight these last few months.
DOCTOR: (work) _____ a lot?

MR. SMITH: Yes, I (work) ——————— at least eleven hours a day since July.

DOCTOR: And how much ——————— (smoke)?

MR. SMITH: I (smoke) ——————— about three packs of cigarettes a day.

DOCTOR: And what kinds of food (eat) ——————— lately?

MR. SMITH: I (eat) ——————— mostly sandwiches for lunch and dinner.

DOCTOR: (take) ——————— that medicine I prescribed?

MR. SMITH: No, Doctor. I've been too busy.

DOCTOR: Well, you'd better take care of yourself, Mr. Smith, or you'll end up in the hospital very soon.

II. You are sure that somebody has been in your apartment and used your things during your absence. From the following evidence, what has this "somebody" been doing?

Example: Some books that were on your shelf are now on the table.

Somebody has been taking books off my shelf.

1. Your record player doesn't work properly.
2. There is a cigarette burn on the arm of the sofa.
3. The papers on your desk are all disorganized.
4. The refrigerator door is open.
5. Your photograph album is on the table.
6. The drawers in your bedroom are all open, and the contents are in a mess.
7. Your phone bill is unusually high this month.
8. Your towels are wet.
9. The TV dial is not on the usual channel.
10. A pair of pants and a shirt that you left in the closet are now on your bed.
11. There are blond hairs in your brush. You have brown hair.
12. A pot of coffee that you left full is now empty.

III. Write a letter to a friend of yours apologizing for not having written sooner. Explain that you've been busy lately and tell your friend what you've been doing.

DISCUSSION

I. Below you will find a list of common diseases and their symptoms. Working in pairs, student 1 should take the part of a doctor, and student 2, the part of a patient. The "patient" should choose one of the diseases below and begin by giving the doctor one or two symptoms. The doctor will continue the interview by asking questions until he diagnoses the disease.

appendicitis

—pain on right side of stomach
—loss of appetite
—vomiting
—low fever

hepatitis

—loss of appetite
—vomiting
—pain in right side of stomach
—fever
—chills
—yellow skin

low blood pressure

—weakness
—tiredness
—headaches
—fast heartbeat
—trouble breathing

diabetes

—headaches
—hunger
—thirst
—skin irritations

sinusitis

—headache (worse at the end of the day)
—pain in the face above or below the eyes
—stuffed up nose

Example: DOCTOR: What seems to be your problem?
PATIENT: Well, Doctor, I've been getting terrible headaches lately.
DOCTOR: Have you had any fever?
PATIENT: No, but I've been getting pains above and below my eyes.
DOCTOR: Well, it looks like a case of sinusitis.

II. Bill and Rosemary's separation was not successful. Some separations have the opposite effect, making two people feel closer emotionally. There are two popular sayings in English: "Absence makes the heart grow fonder" and "Out of sight, out of mind." Which do you believe is true?

BITS AND PIECES

I. *How about . . . . -ing?*
The expression *How about . . . . -ing* means the same as *Let's . . . ,* and is used when the speaker wants to suggest an activity.

Example: How about going to a movie?

Mr. and Mrs. Benson are planning to celebrate their fiftieth wedding anniversary next week. Mrs. Benson is suggesting things they might do, and Mr. Benson is agreeing.

With the cues below, create dialogues between the Bensons using *How about . . . -ing?* Begin Mr. Benson's response with *That's a good idea! It's been such a long time since I . . .*

Example: that new disco

MRS. BENSON: How about going to that new disco?

MR. BENSON: That's a good idea! It's been such a long time since I went dancing.

1. that Verdi opera
2. that nice French restaurant
3. a bottle of champagne
4. a car trip to Niagara Falls
5. the new casino

6. the afternoon at the tennis club
7. the grandchildren in California
8. the weekend at the beach
9. a picnic in the country
10. to Acapulco for the weekend

II. *I haven't done that in (for) ages*
   in (for) ages is an expression used to convey the idea of a very long period of time.

Example: I haven't seen him in (for) ages.

Using the cues for the previous exercise, make sentences with *in (for) ages* and the present perfect (negative).

Example: that new disco

MRS. BENSON: How about going to that new disco?

MR. BENSON: That's a good idea! I haven't gone dancing in ages.

PRESENTATION

THE THEFT OF THE CENTURY

Have you ever worked with a gang, Ted?

The Dobson gang is planning to steal the famous "Mona Lisa" from the Louvre Museum. Mike Dobson is interviewing a candidate for the job. He wants to know about Ted's experience. Ted has had very little experience.

—with a gang	(*work*)	—a walkie-talkie	(*use*)
—a job like this	(*do*)	—a brick wall	(*climb*)
—an alarm system	(*shut off*)	—a building	(*break into*)
—a gun	(*carry*)	—the Louvre Museum	(*visit*)
—a getaway car	(*drive*)	—the "Mona Lisa"	(*see*)
—arrested	(*be*)		

I. Taking the parts of Mike Dobson and Ted, ask and answer questions using the above cues.

Example: DOBSON: Have you ever worked with a gang, Ted?
TED: Well, no, I haven't, but I'm willing to learn.

II. Ted was hired to do the job. He has sixteen minutes to break into the museum and replace the "Mona Lisa" with a fake while the guards are changing. Dobson is outside with a walkie-talkie and the following checklist. Re-create their conversation using the checklist.

Example: DOBSON: Have you cut the alarm wires yet?
TED: a) Yes, I have.
    b) No, I haven't cut them yet, but I'm just about to.
    c) No, I still haven't cut them, but I'm just about to.

> *Checklist*
>
> 1. 12:00—cut alarm wires
> 2. 12:03—climb wall of right wing
> 3. 12:06—open bathroom window
> 4. 12:08—go down corridor
> 5. 12:09—hide behind curtains
> 6. 12:10—guard leaves room
> 7. 12:11—guard goes down corridor
> 8. 12:12—enter room
> 9. 12:13—take away protective ropes
> 10. 12:14—take "Mona Lisa" off the wall
> 11. 12:15—put fake on the wall
> 12. 12:16—new guard comes on duty

III. The police have been trying to catch the Dobson gang for years. They know about the plan to steal the "Mona Lisa," and through electronic surveillance, they are watching every move Ted makes. Inspector Klutz of Interpol is reporting back to headquarters.

Example   INSPECTOR KLUTZ: OK, boys, he's already cut the alarm wires and now he's about to climb the wall.

Continue the report, referring to the checklist.

EXPANSION

Read the following short story.

Confidence Man

"I've never been so humiliated in my life!" shouted Dorothy angrily. "Why didn't you stand up to that jerk? Tell me," she continued, "have you *ever* lost your temper or been in a fight? I'll bet you've never hit anybody in your whole life!"

"How would you like to be the first?" Clyde said to himself, knowing that Dorothy couldn't hear him. She was walking rapidly away in the direction of the parking lot.

The next day at work, Clyde couldn't help thinking about the incident. They had been relaxing on the beach when Dorothy decided she was hungry. At the refreshment stand, a big muscular man had pushed in front of them and stepped on Dorothy's foot. Clyde had made a weak protest, but the man had only laughed in his face.

His thoughts were suddenly interrupted when the manager shouted, "Clyde! Have you waited on that customer yet? I've got a business to run here, so wake up, will you? And what about the inventory list? Have you taken it to Mr. Watson yet?" Not even waiting for a reply, the manager hurried back to his office. "I'm tired of this!" Clyde whispered, knowing his boss couldn't hear him.

That evening Clyde was reading the newspaper when he saw an advertisement: DO YOU LACK SELF-CONFIDENCE? HAVE YOU EVER FELT UNPOPULAR AND LEFT OUT OF A GROUP? IF YOU HAVEN'T ENROLLED YET, ENROLL NOW IN DOCTOR IVO'S CONFIDENCE COURSE. AFTER A FEW EASY LESSONS YOU'LL BE A DIFFERENT PERSON."

"That's just what I need," Clyde thought. "I'll enroll tomorrow."

After finishing the course, Clyde really did feel like a new person. When Dorothy finally called him, he decided to show off his new personality. "Clyde! I haven't heard from you in ages! Why don't we go and see the new movie at the Roxy?" "I've already seen it," Clyde said confidently. "I took Linda to see it last night, as a matter of fact."

Dorothy was shocked. "You've already seen it, have you?" she said furiously. "Yes, I have," said Clyde calmly. "If I have time I might give you a call next week, but I haven't made up my mind yet," he said, hanging up the phone.

The next day at work his boss started shouting at him as usual, but this time Clyde answered, "Listen, Mr. Bumstern, I've already written that report and given it to Mr. Watson. In fact, it's only eleven o'clock, and I've already sold two hundred dollars' worth of merchandise, so why don't you shout at somebody else for a change?"

Two months later, Clyde was sitting in the company lunch room with his friends, telling jokes and flirting confidently with all the girls. "Mr. Bumstern told us that you've already broken last year's sales record," said Frank, a fellow worker, "and this fiscal year hasn't even ended yet!" "Have you ever thought of selling your secret of success to the rest of us?" asked Miriam, the cashier.

Clyde smiled and told his story—his feelings of rejection, and the confidence he gained with Doctor Ivo. "Ivo, Ivo," repeated Miriam; "I've never heard of him." "I have," said Frank. "Haven't you seen the article about him in the newspaper yet, Clyde?" He pulled out *The Daily Mail* and pointed to the article: CON MAN WALLACE IVO CONVICTED OF FRAUD. Clyde read the article with a sick feeling in his stomach.

"Forget that dumb article and tell us a joke," said Miriam. Everyone smiled and waited eagerly for Clyde to tell them one of his funny stories. "I can't . . . uh . . . I mean . . . I've never . . . I can't remember . . . I mean I've never been able to tell good jokes." He got up and left the table.

Not long afterwards, Clyde lost his job. He hadn't made a single sale in three months. "You're a funny guy," said Mr. Bumstern when he fired him. "I've never met anyone like you. What you need is a confidence course. Have you ever thought of taking one?" "No, sir, I never have." Clyde smiled sadly, picked up his briefcase, and walked out into the rain.

I. Complete the following using *never, ever, already,* and *yet.*

<u>*Never*</u>

I _____ so humiliated in my whole life.   *(be)*
I'll bet you _____ anybody in your life.   *(hit)*
I _____ of him.   *(hear)*
I _____ to tell jokes.   *(be able)*
I _____ anyone like you.   *(meet)*

<u>*Ever*</u>

_____ you_____ your temper?   *(lose)*
_____ you_____ of selling your   *(think)*
secret of success to the rest of us?
_____ you_____ unpopular and   *(feel)*
left out of a group?
_____ you_____ of taking a confi-   *(think)*
dence course?

<u>*Already*</u>

I _____ it   *(see)*
I _____ that report   *(write)*
I _____ two hundred dollars' worth of   *(sell)*
merchandise
You _____ last year's sales record   *(break)*

<u>*Yet*</u>

interrogative: _____ you _____ on   *(wait)*
that customer _____?
_____ you_____ that   *(take)*
report to Mr. Watson _____?
_____ you_____ that   *(see)*
article _____?
_____ you_____ in   *(enroll)*
that course _____?
negative: This fiscal year _____.   *(end)*

II. Working in pairs, choose one of the following sets of characters and have an informal conversation. Use information from the story as well as ideas of your own. You may want to make written notes in order to perform your conversation later for the rest of the class.

1. Clyde—Dorothy
2. Clyde—Mr. Bumstern
3. Clyde—Doctor Ivo
4. Clyde—Frank

GRAMMAR SUMMARY

EVER, NEVER, ALREADY, YET

These time expressions are used with the present perfect to indicate past actions whose precise time is not stated.

I. Ever/Never

    A. *Ever* is used in questions and has the meaning of "at any time in your/her/etc., life?" Its position is before the past participle.

Examples: Have you *ever* seen an elephant?
Has Joan *ever* eaten Hungarian goulash?

    B. *Never* is used in negations and means "at no point in my/your/etc., life." It is also placed before the past participle.

Examples: I've *never* seen such a beautiful apartment.
He's *never* driven a car.

    C. The expression *before* is often used with both *ever* and *never* with the meaning of "before now." It goes at the end of the sentence.

Examples: Have you ever worked with him *before?*
I've never seen him *before.*

II. Already

    Already is used in affirmative sentences and has the meaning of "previously" or "by or before the time of speaking." Its position is before the past participle.

Examples: I've already called the police.
They've already chosen the winner.
He's already made three mistakes.

III. Yet

    A. *Yet—interrogative. Yet* is used in questions and is placed at the end of the sentence.

Examples: Has he bought a new car *yet?*
Have you packed your bags *yet?*

    B. i. *Yet—negative. Yet* is used in negations and means "up to now" or "so far." It is usually placed at the end of the sentence.

Examples: We haven't made any definite plans *yet.*
The train hasn't left *yet.*

      ii. The word *still* can also be used in negations as an alternative to yet, but it is placed before the verb. *Still* emphasizes the fact that the action has not occurred and implies that it should have already occurred.

Examples: He *still* hasn't paid for the tickets.

They *still* haven't called the police.

Notes

i. The use of *just* to express a recently completed action is normally used with the simple past tense in American English, although British usage requires it to be accompanied by the present perfect.

Examples: I just finished eating.
(British—I've just finished eating)

ii. American English often uses the simple past tense to accompany *ever, never, already,* and *yet* instead of the present perfect.

Examples: Did you ever see that TV program?
(Have you ever seen that TV program?)

I never rode a horse in my life.
(I've never ridden a horse in my life.)

I already saw that movie.
(I've already seen that movie.)

Did you eat lunch yet?
(Have you eaten lunch yet?)

iii. The verb *be* is often used instead of the verb *go* when the meaning is "go and return."

Examples: Have you ever been to Paris?

They've already been to the police.

iv. *Already* and *yet* may be implicit in the sentence, even though they are they are not stated. In these cases the present perfect is still used.

Examples: Have you paid the bill (yet)?

Yes, I've (already) paid it.

INTENSIVE PRACTICE

I. Complete the following questions using *yet* and the verbs in parentheses.

Example: Janis/those letters?   *(type)*
Has Janis typed those letters yet?

1. you/to your friend?	*(write)*
2. Tom/a job?	*(find)*
3. they/lunch?	*(have)*
4. your brother/his homework?	*(do)*
5. Mr. Wilson/his new suit?	*(wear)*

6. you/your medicine?   (*take*)
7. he/the police?   (*call*)
8. Mrs. Jones/her car?   (*sell*)
9. you/the film at the Roxy?   (*see*)
10. she/the telephone bill?   (*pay*)

II. Complete the following using *ever* and an appropriate verb.

Example: _____ she _____ the measles?

Has she ever had the measles?

1. _____ you_____ in a jet plane?
2. _____ John _____ a love poem?
3. _____ they_____ a play by Ionesco?
4. _____ I_____ a lie?
5. _____ you_____ such a beautiful girl?
6. _____ he_____ Chinese food?
7. _____ Mary_____ in jail?
8. _____ they_____ to the President before?
9. _____ we_____ Beethoven's Fifth Symphony?
10. _____ you_____ a cold in the summer?

III. Ask a question with *When . . . going to* and answer it using *already*. Pay close attention to the following example:

Example: your sister/her exam
When is your sister going to take her exam?
She's already taken it.

1. you/call the police
2. they/choose a new car
3. Peter/begin his French course
4. she/read that book
5. you/speak to Martha
6. he/have his operation
7. Laura/feed the baby
8. Tom/pay his bills
9. Janet/do the dishes
10. Peter and Liz/give a party

IV. Complete the following sentences with the negative and *yet*. Use the words in parentheses.

Example: I've been looking for my glasses for three days, but I . . . . (*find them*)
I've been looking for my glasses for three days, but I haven't found them yet.

1. I bought a new tie the other day, but I   (*wear it*)
   _____

2. I've been on a diet for two weeks, but I   (*lose any weight*)
   _____

3. I took fifty dollars out of the bank last week, *(spend it)*
   but I _____

4. I bought a new book the other day, but I *(read it)*
   _____

5. He's been driving a car for twenty years and *(have an accident)*
   he _____

6. He's been promising her a diamond ring for *(give her one)*
   ages, but he _____

7. Mr. Weeks bought a new car last week, but *(drive it)*
   his wife _____

8. The baby has been in bed for an hour, but he *(fall asleep)*
   _____

9. My sister's birthday is tomorrow, but I *(buy her a present)*
   _____

10. He gave me a box of chocolates, but I *(eat them all)*
    _____

V. Complete the following sentences using a contraction + *never*. Follow
the example.

Example: We _____ such a delicious salad, _____ ?
We've never eaten such a delicious salad, have we?

1. They _____ such beautiful music, _____ ?
2. You _____ such a terrible lie before, _____ ?
3. Margaret _____ to such a luxurious restaurant, _____ ?
4. Jack _____ such a bad movie, _____ ?
5. They _____ such a long letter before, _____ ?
6. We _____ such a bad book, _____ ?
7. Mary and Wayne _____ such a long trip before, _____ ?
8. She _____ in such a fast train before, _____ ?
9. He _____ to such a big city before, _____ ?
10. You _____ on such a soft bed before, _____ ?

VI. When Buster Biggs was campaigning for mayor of Midville, he made
lots of campaign promises that he hasn't kept yet. Referring to the following campaign slogans and the time element beside each, complain
about Mayor Biggs's lack of action, using *still* and the present perfect.

Example: "Buster Biggs will get rid of organized crime!" (City Hall—1978)
He's been in City Hall since 1978, and he still hasn't gotten rid of organized
crime.

1. "Buster Biggs will build a modern, totally equipped high school!"
   (mayor—4 years)
2. "Buster Biggs will make it safe to walk down the streets at night!"
   (running the local government—a long time)
3. "Buster Biggs will do away with pollution!"
   (in charge—ages)
4. "Buster Biggs will get Midville a new hospital!"
   (making promises—1965)

5. "Buster Biggs will put Midville on the map!"
   (in power—years)
6. "Buster Biggs will find investment for local industry!"
   (earning a high salary—1970)
7. "Buster Biggs will put an end to corruption!"
   (controlling things—1978)
8. "Buster Biggs will keep all his promises!"
   (managing things—years)

WRITING AND HOMEWORK

I. Fill in the blanks:

1. Would you like to join us for lunch? No thanks. I _____
   already_____ .
2. She's getting married next week but she _____ her wedding
   dress yet.
3. _____ you ever_____ your wife's birthday?
4. _____ your father _____ the newspaper yet?
5. I gave her a beautiful pair of gloves for her birthday, but she still
   _____ them.
6. It's too late! I _____ already _____ the letter.
7. Can you believe it? He _____ never _____ to a concert in his life!
8. _____ they ever _____ champagne?
9. He's leaving for Paris tomorrow, but he still _____ his bags.
10. I _____ never _____ to Scotland, but I'd like to go
    there someday.

II. The following story is not in logical order. First fill in the blanks and then
    rearrange the eight small sections to form a logical narrative.

—"Robbery! I _____ never _____ (steal) anything in my
  life! I'm an honest guy! I'm calling my lawyer right now! Let me out
  of here!" shouted Donovan.
—"_____ you ever_____ (be) to the Purple Dragon Bar,
  Donovan?" asked one of the detectives.
—"I _____ never _____ (see) that man before in my life!"
  insisted Donovan. "Why are you asking all these questions? What did
  I do?"
—Last Wednesday night, the police arrested Bill Donovan and took
  him to headquarters for questioning. Donovan, of course, didn't want
  to tell them anything.
—"Sit down, Donovan. You're not going anywhere!" said the detective.
  "We _____ already _____ (hire) a lawyer for you, and
  it looks like you're going to need one."

—"No! Never," said Donovan. "I _____ never even _____ (hear of) a bar by that name.

—"We have reason to believe that you and this man were involved in a robbery," said the detective.

—"But we _____ already _____ (talk to) several people who say they saw you at the Purple Dragon Bar having a drink with this man," said the detective, showing him a photograph.

II. Mr. and Mrs. Anderson went on a brief vacation and left their two teen-aged children in charge of the house. They arrived home unexpectedly, however, and have just phoned from the airport. "We'll be home in about half an hour," said Mrs. Anderson.

Bob and Joanne are in a panic because the house is a mess.

Example: BOB: They'll be here in less than half an hour. Have you done the dishes yet?

JOANNE: No, I haven't. What about the beds? Have you made them yet?

Using questions with *yet,* write the rest of the conversation as Bob and Joanne talk about:

—vacuum the living room carpet
—take out the garbage
—dust the furniture
—hide the broken mirror
—empty the ash trays
—give the dog a bath
—water the plants

III. Buster Biggs's Speech

"Fellow citizens: I know that many of you have accused me of not taking direct action. 'Where's the new hospital?' you say, 'and the new recreation center? What about the gangsters you promised to put in jail, and the rent control law you promised to introduce? What about your promise to raise the salaries of city employees and the credit you promised to extend to local farmers?'

"But what about my achievements? Yes, what about them? In three short years our city has seen the building of a new library and a city hall. I promised to get ten million dollars in outside investments for local industry and I did. Yes, ladies and gentlemen, I promised to clean up our streets and get rid of pollution—and I did. I promised to lower the rate of unemployment and control inflation, and I did—all in three years.

"Fellow citizens, this criticism is unjustified. It's true that I still have many things to do, but look at what I have already done for Midville!"

Write a dialogue between a Buster Biggs supporter and a supporter of his opponent. Use the facts in Buster Biggs's speech to discuss what he has done and what he hasn't done.

Example: A: Well, I say Buster is great! He's only been mayor for three years and he's already built a new city library!

B: Okay, but he still hasn't built the hospital—and we certainly need a hospital more than a library.

Continue the conversation.

DISCUSSION

I. A "confidence man" (con man) is one who cheats people out of their money after winning their confidence. He sometimes gets people to spend thousands of dollars by telling them lies and inventing schemes that sound true.

Pretend you are a con man. Persuade a classmate to do the following:

1. spend two thousand dollars to buy the Brooklyn Bridge
2. buy shares in Atlas Computers (a fictitious company)
3. donate fifty dollars to the Sinusitis Foundation (a fictitious foundation), which is dedicated to ending this disease
4. donate money toward the invention of a fuel pill, a substitute for gasoline
5. donate money toward financing an expedition to study plant life at the North Pole

II. There is going to be an election in the following cities. The mayors of these cities have made important improvements but there are still many problems to solve. Carry on a debate between the two candidates running for the position of mayor. One student should take the part of the present mayor campaigning for re-election. He will talk about his main achievement. Another student will be his opponent. He will talk about the city's major problem. Take a few minutes to prepare what you are going to say.

Cities	Problems	Achievements
Midville	high crime rate	improved garbage collection
Longborough	highest pollution level in the U.S.	new cultural center
Old York	dying industry	new hospital
Springton	poor housing	new public education
Morely	unemployment	more public housing
Clarkton	no parks or gardens	decrease in taxes
Hackburgh	poor roads and highways	new university

BITS AND PIECES

I. *What does she/he look like?*
The expression *What does she/he look like?* is used when you want to get a physical description.

WANTED
MIKE DOBSON

HEIGHT—5'8"
WEIGHT—150 lbs.
AGE—49
EYES—BROWN
HAIR—BALD
DISTINGUISHING FEATURES:
SCAR ON FOREHEAD,
BEARD, BIG EARS

WANTED
TED HARRIS

HEIGHT—6'
WEIGHT—180 lbs.
AGE—22
EYES—BLUE
HAIR—BLOND
DISTINGUISHING FEATURES:
GLASSES, BROKEN FRONT
TOOTH, CURLY HAIR

WANTED
ANGELA NYE

HEIGHT—5'2"
WEIGHT—118 lbs.
AGE—32
EYES—DARK BROWN
HAIR—DARK BROWN
DISTINGUISHING FEATURES:
LONG NECK, BEAUTY
MARK ON RIGHT CHEEK

The police are trying to catch the Dobson gang. The above "wanted" posters have been put up in all public buildings. People who think they have seen the criminals are calling the police station.

Using the information on the posters, take the parts of Inspector Klutz and a telephone caller who thinks he(she) has seen Mike, Ted, or Angela. Klutz begins with: What does he(she) look like? and then asks for a more detailed description.

Example: CALLER: I think I've seen Mike Dobson.
KLUTZ: What does he look like?
CALLER: Well, he's average height and is bald.
KLUTZ: What color are his eyes?
CALLER: I don't remember.
KLUTZ: About how old is he?

Now continue the conversation.

II. *What is she/he like?*

The expression *What is he(she) like?* is used to ask for information about someone's personality.

Working in pairs and using the information in the *Writing and Homework* section of Chapter 8, ask questions and give information about relatives and friends. Use *What is he(she) like?*, or the contraction, *What's he(she) like?*

Example: STUDENT A: My father is a Capricorn.
STUDENT B: What's he like?
STUDENT A: Well he's not ambitious like most Capricorns, but he *is* conservative.

PRESENTATION

WENDY STORM'S BAD YEAR

I've broken only five contracts this year.

Wendy Storm, the famous movie actress, has had a bad year and her career is suffering. Fame has gone to her head, making her unreliable, temperamental, and careless with her money. Her agent is trying to make her see how different this year has been in comparison with last year.

I. Re-create the dialogue between Wendy and her agent, using the following cues:

		Last Year	*This Year*
How many?			
contracts	*(break)*	1	5
movies	*(make)*	4	1
fan letters	*(get)*	500,000	3,000
rehearsals	*(miss)*	2	15

How many times?			
with co-stars	(*fight*)	0	14
late for work	(*be*)	1	dozens
home early	(*go*)	2	30 or more
with the director	(*argue*)	1	20

How much?			
money	(*make*)	$2 million	$50,000
money	(*spend*)	$200,000	$200,000
money	(*save*)	$1.8 million	0
weight	(*gain*)	0	30 lbs.

Example: AGENT: Wendy, don't you see you're destroying your career? How many contracts did you break last year?

WENDY: I broke only one contract last year—the one with International Studios.

AGENT: And how many contracts have you broken this year?

WENDY: Well, so far I've broken five—but it's because I didn't like the directors.

Continue the dialogue using the information above. Add your own comments whenever possible.

II. Imagine a dialogue between Wendy and her director. They are comparing this week and last week. Talk about: coffee breaks (*have*); sedatives (*take*); money at the casino (*lose*); her lines (*forget*); cigarettes (*smoke*); parties (*go to*).

EXPANSION

I. Read the following play, taking the parts of the characters: David Snow, Wendy, Fred, Jack, Ray, Florence, Ted.

Faces in Focus

DAVID SNOW: Good evening ladies and gentlemen. Tonight on *Faces in Focus* my lovely co-host, Wendy Storm, and I would like to welcome five fantastic record breakers!

WENDY: Yes, these fine people are all trying to break very different kinds of records. Let's talk to our first guest. Mr. Fred Appleby—well known to tennis fans everywhere.

DAVID: Fred, you've been a tennis champ for a long time, but this year has been a special one for you, hasn't it?

FRED: Yes, David. I've played in forty tournaments so far this year, and I've won all of them.

WENDY: You've also broken the money-making record, haven't you?

FRED: Yes, Wendy, I've won three million dollars this year.

DAVID: And how much did you win last year, Fred?

FRED: Well, last year I won only a million dollars. Quite a big improvement, wouldn't you say?

WENDY: Yes—but you know you're not the only one with a lot of endurance, Fred. Jack Lawson here has had a tough year too. I understand you're trying to break the world's record for long distance walking, Jack?

JACK: That's right, Wendy.

DAVID: How many miles have you walked so far this year?

JACK: Well, I've walked about 2,000 miles so far, and there are still three months to go before the end of the year.

DAVID: How many different places have you been to during the course of your walks, Jack?

JACK: I've been to seven different European countries, and I've walked across fifteen states in the U.S. But it's been really hard!

WENDY: What do you mean, Jack?

JACK: So far this year I've been to the hospital seven times with foot trouble. I've been attacked by thieves, chased by dogs, insulted by the press, and . . . well, I've lost about twenty-five pounds, too.

DAVID: Well, here's a man who probably hasn't lost any weight, right, Ray? It's Ray Campbell, pancake champ!

RAY: That's right, David. Excuse me for talking with my mouth full, but I can't afford to lose any time.

DAVID: Ray is trying to break the twenty-four-hour pancake-eating record. How many pancakes have you eaten so far today?

RAY: About 400. I tried to break the record last year, too, but I only managed to eat 350.

WENDY: How much weight do you think you've gained in the last few hours?

RAY: Well, I've eaten 400 pancakes, ten pounds of butter, and two gallons of syrup. So, I've probably gained about twenty-five pounds today. Excuse me while I take another bite.

WENDY: That's quite all right, Ray. And now Florence Castro. What record are you trying to break, Florence?

FLORENCE: I'm hoping to break the uninterrupted gum-chewing record. I've been chewing gum without stopping for eight months.

DAVID: Even in your sleep?

FLORENCE: Yes, David, I even chew in my sleep. It becomes a reflex action after a while. I figure I've chewed about 550 packs of gum this year. I've spent hundreds of dollars on gum, and also on vitamins to supplement my diet.

WENDY: How many times have you been to the dentist this year, Florence?

FLORENCE: I haven't been to the dentist at all this year. I'd be afraid to see the bill.

DAVID: Amazing! And now for our last guest, Ted Doolittle. Ted is trying to break the most unusual record of all, a truly fantastic attempt that requires courage and stamina. It's just amazing!

WENDY: It certainly is! Many have tried before and failed. Tell us about your record, Ted.

TED: Well, despite inflation and the high cost of living, I've gone ten years without giving my employees a raise.

(All gasp, and Florence chokes on her gum.)

II. The next day, David Snow had some more record breakers on his TV show. Take the parts of David, Wendy, and the following guests that they interview. You may want to make notes of what you plan to say.

a. a champion typist
b. a marathon runner
c. a fisherman
d. an encyclopedia salesman
e. a mountain climber
f. an antique car collector

GRAMMAR SUMMARY

UNFINISHED TIME AND THE PRESENT PERFECT

I. The present perfect is used with such words and phrases as *today, this week, this month,* and *this year* to convey the idea of an unfinished period of time.

Examples: I've eaten only one meal today.

She hasn't spent much money this week.

Have they been to the casino this month?

II. If a definite time in the past is stated (*yesterday, last week, last month,* etc.) the simple past tense must be used, *not* the present perfect.

Examples: I ate only one meal yesterday.
She didn't spend much money last week.
Did they go to the casino last month?

III. *How much/many?* and *How many times?*

Information questions with *How much, How many,* and *How many times* are used with both the present perfect and the simple past tense. When information questions are asked with the present perfect, the speaker is referring to an unfinished period of time. When questions with the simple past tense are asked, the speaker is referring to a finished period of time.

Example: How much milk have you had today? — unfinished period of time (today)
I've had three glasses.

How much milk did you have yesterday? — finished period of time (yesterday)
I had five glasses.

How many books have you read this month?
I've read six.

How many books did you read last month?
I read two.

How many times has she brushed her teeth today?
She's brushed them twice.

How many times did she brush her teeth yesterday?
She brushed them three times.

INTENSIVE PRACTICE

I. Complete the following questions beginning with *How much* or *How many.* Answer the questions using the information in parentheses.

Example: money/save/this year ($500.00)

How much money have you saved this year?
I've saved $500.00

lies/tell/today? (0)

How many lies have you told today?
I haven't told any.

1. milk/have today?	(4 glasses)
2. books/read this month?	(2)
3. cigarettes/smoke today?	(0)
4. classes/miss this week?	(1)
5. letters/write this week?	(3)
6. money/earn this year?	(a lot)
7. pills/take today?	(0)
8. miles/walk this week?	(6)
9. fruit/eat today?	(2 bananas)
10. weight/lose this month?	(0)

II. Complete the following questions using *How many times + be.* Answer the questions in the negative + *at all.*

Example: you/to the movies this week?

How many times have you been to the movies this week?
I haven't been to the movies at all this week.

1. they/to the dentist this month?
2. she/in the hospital this year?
3. Mrs. Davis/to the supermarket today?
4. Bob/to New York this year?
5. you/to the doctor this month?

III. Complete the following questions, beginning with *How many times.* Answer them using . . . *only* . . . *once.*

Example: he/try to quit smoking this year?

How many times has he tried to quit smoking this year?
He's only tried to quit smoking once.

1. you/brush your teeth today?
2. he/wash his hair this week?
3. she/answer the phone this morning?
4. you/be late for work this week?
5. she/miss the train this month?

IV. Complete the following questions and answers.

Example: yesterday she/write two postcards   today/any

Yesterday she wrote two postcards, but today she hasn't written any.

yesterday they/buy three newspapers   today/only one

Yesterday they bought three newspapers, but today they've bought only one.

1. last month I/lose two pounds	this month/only one
2. last week she/spend two hundred dollars	this week/only fifty dollars
3. last month they/give three parties	this month/any
4. yesterday she/drink four cups of tea	today/only one
5. last week he/teach seven lessons	this week/only three
6. yesterday he/steal two wallets	today/only one
7. last month they/win four games	this month/any
8. last year he/have three car accidents	this year/any
9. yesterday I/eat three apples	today/only one
10. last month I/borrow a lot of money	this month/any

V. Imagine what each of the following characters might say.
Use the present perfect with an unfinished time period.

Example: worried parents
He's only phoned us once this month.

1. a bad student	6. a busy typist
2. a hungry person	7. a successful salesman
3. a busy taxi driver	8. a worried restaurant owner
4. an unsuccessful policeman	9. a person on a diet
5. a heavy smoker	10. a successful writer

WRITING AND HOMEWORK

I. Fill in the blanks.

1. She _____ three books last month, but she _____ (negative) any this month.
2. How many times _____ he _____ late for work this week?
3. He _____ two aspirins so far today, but he _____ (negative) any yesterday.
4. _____ they _____ a lot of money this month?
5. How many times _____ you _____ your teeth yesterday?
6. I _____ (negative) to the movies at all this month.
7. Bob _____ three exams so far this week.
8. I _____ to the doctor twice this year.
9. He _____ (negative) any work so far today, and he _____ (negative) any work yesterday either.
10. Professor Biggins _____ two lessons yesterday.

II. Complete the following dialogue:
Mr. and Mrs. Billings, a wealthy couple, have spent far too much money this year. Mr. Billings is talking to his accountant.

MANAGER: Yes, Mr. Billings. Your financial situation is quite serious. You _____ a lot of money this year.

BILLINGS: Do you really think so? I mean, I thought I was being careful. For instance, I _____ only _____ one new car this year, and we _____ any new servants at all.

MANAGER: That may be true, but how many cocktail parties _____ this month?

BILLINGS: Well, let's see. We _____ four or five, but my wife insists that we have to keep up our social standing.

MANAGER: Speaking of your wife, Mr. Billings, she _____ $2000 on clothes last month, and she _____ already _____ $1000 this month.

BILLINGS: Yes, I'll have a word with her. But listen, we *are* trying to save money. We used to go to the opera every week. This month we _____ to the opera *or* to the theater at all. We _____ even _____ a vacation this year.

MANAGER: Getting back to your wife, Mr. Billings; she _____ lunch with her women's club almost every day this week at the Chez Ritz restaurant. According to my figures, she _____ almost $800 last month on expensive lunches.

BILLINGS: You know, I _____ any money at all on clothes or expensive lunches this month.

MANAGER: Well, perhaps you and your wife ought to have a talk about this situation.

BILLINGS: Tell me, how much does a divorce cost?

III. Ricky Lander, the famous racing driver, was interviewed by *Auto World* magazine. This year has been better for Ricky than last year. Write an article about Ricky comparing last year with this year, which is still not over. Use the following information in your article:

	Last Year	*This Year*
Races entered	9 (5 Grand Prix)	12 (8 Grand Prix)
Races won	5	10
Cars driven	Ferrari	Ferrari; McLaren
Miles driven	5,000	6,000
Average m.p.h.	145	155
Money won	$300,000	$500,000
Accidents	2	1

Begin: This has been a good year for Ricky Lander. Last year Ricky entered nine races, five of which were Grand Prix. This year so far he has entered twelve major races, eight of which were Grand Prix. . . .

DISCUSSION

I. About record breakers:
Six well-known psychiatrists appeared on David Snow's *Faces in Focus* to discuss record breaking. Here are some of the psychiatrists' comments. Which ones do you agree/disagree with? Give your reasons.

1. "A person who is willing to eat a hundred hot dogs in an hour, swallow fifty goldfish, or stay under water for six minutes is simply trying to kill himself. The record breaker is simply trying to fulfill a death wish."

2. "The real object of the dance marathon—a contest in which a couple would dance for days—was simply the love of money. People will subject themselves to almost anything just to win a few dollars."

3. "What motivates the record breaker is the chance to be immortal. We all want to be famous. People who try to break bizarre records are just mediocre individuals with no special talents who can find no other way to win fame and immortality except by doing strange things."

4. "In my day, it was the fashion to see how many goldfish you could swallow or how long you could sit on top of a flagpole. In the fifties the craze was to see how many people you could fit into a phone booth. If you ask me, it just proves that there will always be mentally unbalanced people. People have to be mentally unbalanced to do things like that."

5. "The increase in the number of bizarre records broken each year is simple to explain. It is the fault of modern society, which promotes excess in everything."

6. "A record breaker in sports is one thing. A breaker of bizarre records is another. An athlete who breaks records is trying to achieve perfection. The other person is just trying to make his stupidity public."

II. GLENDA: Sure, I've broken a record. I waited four hours the other day to see my doctor!

MARIA: That's nothing! I once waited fifteen hours in Kennedy Airport to catch a flight to Bangkok!

STACY: Big deal! My brother and I had a bet to see who could eat the most hamburgers, and I ate four!

ALEX: And I got the lowest mark on a Chemistry exam—a 35!

We all have broken *personal* records. Discuss some of your personal records.

BITS AND PIECES

It depends on whether (or not)

Whether (or not) can be used instead of the word *if,* in all cases *except* the conditional.

Example: I don't know *if* I can finish my work in time.
I don't know *whether (or not)* I can finish my work in time.

Answer the questions below, using *It depends on whether (or not)* . . .

Example: Are you planning to buy a new car?   (a raise)
I'm not sure. It depends on whether or not my boss gives me a raise.

1. Are you planning to go to the beach tomorrow?   (*rain*)
2. Are you planning to visit your parents in London?   (*a month's vacation*)
3. Are you planning to buy a color TV?   (*enough money*)
4. Are you planning to take tennis lessons?   (*enough time*)
5. Are you planning to ask your boss for a raise today?   (*a good mood*)
6. Are you planning to go to law school?   (*my final exams*)
7. Are you planning to move to Chicago?   (*a better job there*)
8. Are you planning to see the movie tonight?   (*tickets*)
9. Are you planning to get married?   (*my girlfriend's parents*)
10. Are you planning to buy that new dress?   (*a few more pounds*)

PRESENTATION

CLYDE TRIES AGAIN

This guy hasn't been able to keep a job.

Clyde Lackluck has sent in his résumé to the Samson Construction Company in response to a want ad he saw in the newspaper.

I. The personnel director of the Samson Construction Company is talking to his assistant. They are commenting on Clyde's résumé.

Example:
DIRECTOR: What kind of experience has this man had?
ASSISTANT: Well, he's given driving lessons.
DIRECTOR: What driving school did he work for? When did he give driving lessons?
ASSISTANT: He worked for Smithson's Driving School, and he gave lessons from February 1967 to March 1967.

DIRECTOR: Why did he leave?
ASSISTANT: Because he had two accidents in a month.

Continue their conversation using the items in Clyde's résumé.

Example: DIRECTOR: What else has he done?
ASSISTANT: Well, he . . .

II. The personnel director of another company is interviewing Clyde. Take the parts of Clyde and the personnel director and carry on an interview. You may want to incorporate the following questions into your interview:
What other job experience have you had?
Where else have you worked?
How much education have you had?
Who else have you worked for?

Example: DIRECTOR: Well, Mr. Lackluck, what kind of job experience have you had?
CLYDE: I've given driving lessons.
DIRECTOR: Really? Who did you work for?
CLYDE: Smithson's Driving School.
DIRECTOR: How long did you work there?
CLYDE: Well, only for a month.

EXPANSION

Read the following text:

Getting Ahead

Gerald had been a door-to-door salesman for the Ace Vacuum Cleaner Company for ten years. He was good at his job and his boss had even asked him to work in the sales office part-time. But the company was very small, and Gerald knew that he could never be much more than a vacuum cleaner salesman and part-time office worker for the rest of his life.

He was reading the newspaper one evening when he saw an ad: "Wanted—Home Utilities Market Prospector. Dynamic young man with at least ten years' sales experience; some office experience preferable."

Gerald showed his wife the ad. "I've had ten years' sales experience," he said enthusiastically, "and I've also worked in the company's sales office. I'm going to answer this ad!"

"Not only that," said his wife, Agnes, "but you've trained hundreds of new salesmen, you've reorganized the whole accounting department, and you've spent hours working overtime without extra pay. I think it's time for a change."

For the next few days he could think of nothing else. He would no longer be just a simple door-to-door salesman. He would have an important position with an impressive name—Home Utilities Market Prospector! When he received an answer to his application a week later, Gerald was overjoyed. "They want to interview me for the job," he said to Agnes eagerly. He put on his best suit, shined his shoes, and hurried downtown to an address on March Street. The personnel director seemed friendly and asked Gerald several questions about his professional life:

"How many different jobs have you had, Mr. Smith?"

"Well, I've only had one—with the Ace Vacuum Cleaner Company. I've been with them for ten years now."

"And how much sales experience have you had?"

"I've had ten years' sales experience. I've mainly worked as a salesman for the company, although I've also worked part-time in the sales office."

"Why do you want to change jobs?"

"Well, I've been a good salesman for the Ace Vacuum Cleaner Company, but I haven't been able to move up or get a better position there."

"And how's your general health? Have you had any serious illnesses?"

"I've been sick now and then, but nothing serious. In fact, I've never been in the hospital, and I've only missed two or three days of work."

The personnel director smiled at Gerald and said, "I think you're just the man we've been looking for. You can start next week." Gerald's eyes lit up, and a smile of pleasure crossed his face at the thought of starting his new job. Agnes would be so pleased. Finally after all these years he was getting ahead.

As he was leaving, he realized that he hadn't asked the personnel manager for details about his new job. "Oh, by the way, I forgot to ask you. What exactly does a home utilities market prospector do?" Gerald's heart was beating in anticipation. "Oh, didn't you know?" said the director, "I thought everybody did. A home utilities market prospector sells things door-to-door. In your case it'll be vacuum cleaners."

I. Working in pairs, take the parts of Gerald and the personnel director. Concentrate on questions concerning work experience and health.

II. Still working in pairs, conduct an interview for the job as a home utilities market prospector. Use your own personal experience to answer the personnel director's questions. If you haven't had experience in sales, invent qualifications that you think may help you to get the job.

GRAMMAR SUMMARY

UNSPECIFIED TIME AND THE PRESENT PERFECT

I. The Present Perfect Tense
Sentences with the present perfect where no definite time is mentioned emphasize the importance of the action itself rather than when, why, how, etc., it happened. These sentences can also convey the notion of *during my, your, etc., lifetime.*

Examples: I've met a lot of important people.
How many jobs have you had?
Clyde hasn't had much luck.

II. The Simple Past Tense
A. Sentences in which a definite time is mentioned (e.g. *yesterday, last week, three years ago, in 1976, last Friday, etc.*) must be used with the simple past tense and not the present perfect.

Examples: I visited Peter in the hospital yesterday.
I gave up smoking three months ago.
Were you in Paris last July?

B. In questions that solicit precise information about a terminated event, stated or implied, the simple past tense must be used and not the present perfect.

Examples: When were you in Australia?
How much money did they spend last month?
Did you see Mary at the party?

C. A conversation will often begin in the present perfect but immediately change to the simple past as more precise information is solicited and a clear idea of precise time emerges.

Examples: —Hey! There's been an accident!
—No kidding! Was anybody hurt?
—Two people were taken to the hospital.

—They've finally found the document!
—No kidding! Where did they find it?
—They found it under the bed.

—He's left the company.
—When did he leave?
—He left last week.

Notes

How long/How long ago

i. a. *How long* is used with the present perfect continuous if the question refers to past actions continuing into the present. (see Chapter 10)

Example: How long have you been working as a translator? (you are still working as a translator)
I've been working as a translator for three years/since 1977.

b. *How long* is used with the simple past tense when the question refers to a past action that is finished and that does *not* continue into the present.

Examples: How long did you stay at that hotel?
We stayed there for three weeks.

How long were you in Rome?
We were there for two weeks.

ii. *How long ago* Questions with *How long ago* ask about the number of months, years, days, etc., that have gone by since the action or event occurred. They take the simple past tense.

Examples: How long ago did he win the Nobel Prize?
He won it ten years ago.

How long ago were you in the south of France?
I was there five years ago.

INTENSIVE PRACTICE

I. Complete the following questions using the present perfect tense. Remember that the questions are asking about things you've done so far in your life.

Example: How many serious illnesses _____? (have)
How many serious illnesses have you had?

1. How many different jobs _____? (have)
2. How many countries _____? (be to)
3. How many times _____? (be in prison)
4. How many trips _____? (take)
5. How many times _____? (be married)
6. How many books _____? (write)
7. How many different houses _____? (live in)
8. How many car accidents _____? (have)
9. How many languages _____? (study)
10. How many famous people _____? (work with)

II. Wendy Storm has had a very busy life. Tell about what she's done in her lifetime, using the cues provided.

Example: _____ a toy factory.
She has worked in a toy factory.

1. _____ for several newspapers.
2. _____ lingerie in a department store.
3. _____ a model.
4. _____ English to foreign students.

5. _____ around the world several times.
6. _____ several films.
7. _____ on TV shows.
8. _____ divorced five times.
9. _____ several cosmetic operations.
10. _____ three books about her life.

III. Refute each of the following statements using the present perfect in the first part and the simple past tense in the second. Follow the examples given below:

Example: Do you know that Mark has never heard a Beethoven symphony?
But _____._____ the Ninth Symphony just yesterday.
But he has.
He heard the Ninth Symphony just yesterday.

1. Do you know that I've never drunk sherry?
   But _____._____ a glass of sherry just yesterday.
2. Do you know that Harry has never seen a film by Fellini?
   But _____._____ *La Strada* just last week.
3. Do you know that Luisa has never read a play by Shakespeare?
   But _____._____ *Hamlet* just last month.
4. Do you know that Mike and Helen have never eaten a hamburger?
   But _____._____ four hamburgers just last week.
5. Do you know that Marco has never taken a math course?
   But _____._____ one just last semester.
6. Do you know that Bill and Andrea have never been to Europe?
   But _____._____ Luxembourg just last week.
7. Do you know that Marcia has never gone camping?
   But _____._____ just yesterday.
8. Do you know that you've never talked to my brother?
   But _____._____ on the phone just a minute ago.
9. Do you know that you've never told me you loved me?
   But _____._____ just last night.
10. Do you know that Jack and Susan have never been to the city?
    But _____._____ just this afternoon.

IV. The personnel directors of each of the following companies are talking to a job applicant who has no experience in the field. Take the parts of the personnel directors and the applicants. Follow the example given below:

Example: Universal Encyclopedia Company (*job:* sell encyclopedias)

APPLICANT: I'm afraid I have no experience in selling encyclopedias.
PERSONNEL DIRECTOR: I'm sorry, but we're looking for someone who has sold encyclopedias before.

1. Atlas Trucking Company (*job:* drive a truck)
   A: _____.
   P.D: _____.
2. Marigold Babysitting Agency (*job:* take care of children)
   A: _____.
   P.D: _____.

3. The Daily Bugle (*job:* write society articles)

    A: _____ .

    P.D: _____ .

4. Norsville Zoo (*job:* feed lions)

    A: _____ .

    P.D: _____ .

5. Worldwide Travel Agency (*job:* give guided tours of New York)

    A: _____ .

    P.D: _____ .

6. United Elevators (*job:* install elevators)

    A: _____ .

    P.D: _____ .

7. International Language Institute (*job:* teach Portuguese)

    A: _____ .

    P.D: _____ .

8. Stanley Jewelers (*job:* cut diamonds)

    A: _____ .

    P.D: _____ .

9. Globe Telephone and Telegraph Company (*job:* deliver telegrams)

    A: _____ .

    P.D: _____ .

10. Flash Photographers (*job:* take color portraits)

    A: _____ .

    P.D: _____ .

WRITING AND HOMEWORK

I. Complete the following sentences using the present perfect or the simple past tense.

1. I _____ (visit) Bangkok three times. The last time I _____ there was in 1975.

2. How many books _____ (write), Mr. Trumbolt? When _____ you _____ your last book?

3. She _____ (have) an interesting life. She _____ (be) an actress, a fashion model, and she _____ even _____ (take) flying lessons.

4. I'm afraid I _____ (have—negative) much sales experience. However, in 1963 I _____ (work) as a salesman for a few months.

5. DOCTOR: _____ you _____ (have) any serious illnesses?

    PATIENT: I _____ typhoid fever when I was a child.

6. John _____ (work) for several newspapers, but he _____ never _____ (write) sports articles.

7. I'm sorry, but we're looking for someone who _____ (drive) a truck before.

8. I _____ (be) in India in 1976. How long _____ there?
9. He thinks he's important because he _____ (work with) a lot of famous people.
10. Of course I like camping! I _____ (go) camping with some friends just last week. We _____ (have) a marvelous time!

II. 1. Choose from the following companies one that you would like to work for and write a letter introducing yourself and talking about your professional experience. Rather than submitting a résumé, include all necessary information in the letter. You may invent your qualifications if you wish.

Example: Marigold Babysitting Agency: *job—babysitting*

(your address) _____
_____
_____

(today's date) _____

Marigold Babysitting Agency
400 Park Road
Montgomery, Alabama 36104

Dear Sirs:

   I'm writing to you in response to your ad in The Daily Bugle for a babysitter. I am a twenty-year-old student at the International Language Center, where I have been studying for the last two years.

   I've had quite a lot of experience in taking care of children. I've worked for several families on a private basis and I've also had jobs with several babysitting agencies. I worked for the Baby Care Center in 1978 and Children's World in 1979.

   Although I haven't had much experience with infants, I've had a lot of practice in taking care of children between the ages of five and ten.

   I hope to be hearing from you soon.

               Yours sincerely,

                  (your signature)

                  (your name)

Companies

International Language Institue; *job*—teacher of Arabic. 200 West Fourth Street, Montgomery, Alabama 36104

Flash Photographers; *job*—taking photographs. 1588 Dixie Highway, Hollywood, Florida 33022

Mundus Airlines; *job*—ticket sales. 807 Breton Road, Toronto, Ontario, Canada 55108

Hanson Translating and Interpreting Agency; *job*—translator Spanish/English, English/Spanish. 500 Bush Road, Austin, Texas 78710

Samson Construction Company; *job*—engineer. 733 New Lots Avenue, Brooklyn, New York, New York 11201

Bumstern's Hardware; *job*—secretary. 801 Mesa Street, Phoenix, Arizona 85026

2. Write a résumé similar to the one given in Exercise III.

III. The Vineyard Press Publishing Co. is preparing to publish another one of Chef Le Pierre's cookbooks. The editor needs to write some biographical notes to put on the book's jacket. He is looking at Le Pierre's résumé to get an idea of what to write.

RÉSUMÉ

NAME: Louis Le Pierre
DATE OF BIRTH: November 1, 1920
PLACE OF BIRTH: Paris, France
EDUCATION: Diploma—Lycée Pasteur
Diploma—Hélène Thierry Cooking School

JOB EXPERIENCE: <u>Waiter</u>—Chez Lui Restaurant, 1936.
<u>Headwaiter</u>—Chez Lui Restaurant, 1937.
<u>Chef</u>—Chez Lui Restaurant, 1939.
<u>Chef</u>—Paris Nights Restaurant, 1941.
<u>Cooking teacher</u>—St. John's School, 1942.
<u>Organizer</u>—International Food Fair, 1944.
<u>Supervisor</u>—International Food Fair, 1945.

OTHER: appeared on <u>Faces in Focus</u>, 1977.
<u>Chef Le Pierre's Cooking Hour</u>, WYUK–TV, 1977–78
Guest Speaker—Worldwide Food Conference, 1976, 1978, 1979.
Winner: Silver Spoon Award, 1975.
Silver Platter Award, 1977.
Golden Turkey Award, 1979.
Author—<u>Easy Gourmet Meals</u> and <u>Easy Chinese Dishes</u>.

Write the biographical summary of Le Pierre that might appear on a book jacket. Talk about his career, using the present perfect tense for general information, and the simple past tense when you mention a specific date or place.

Example: During his long career, Louis Le Pierre has been a . . .
He organized the International Food Fair in 1977 and . . .

DISCUSSION

I. Read the following newspaper article:

> ### COUNTRY DOCTOR FOUND UNQUALIFIED
>
> The courtroom was overflowing today as the trial of "Dr." Hiram Smith got underway. Smith, who has been practicing medicine in Midville, a small town of 2,000 inhabitants, since 1925, was arrested on Friday when it was discovered that he had falsified his medical qualifications. "I never had a chance to go to medical school. What I wanted most in life was to be a doctor, but my parents were too poor to pay for my education."
>
> Smith, who studied medicine on his own for five years before setting up practice, has been loved and respected by three generations of Midvillagers. "I just don't think it's fair," said one Midville citizen. "He's saved hundreds of lives and knows more about medicine than any of these new doctors with all their degrees."

Take the parts of the following people and organize a discussion.

Example: *For:*   Citizens of Midville (each of whom has a "story" to prove how wonderful Doctor Smith is)

Pamela Plimpton—mother of twins—one had chicken pox, the other had measles, and both were treated by Hiram Smith.

Police Chief Lanagan—shot in the leg. Bullet removed and wound treated by Hiram Smith.

Charlie Holt—broken arm, treated by Hiram Smith.

Against: Representatives of the American Medical Association: Lester Morton, Connie Cook

Jackson Harper—a new doctor who is trying to set up a practice in Midville

II. "It is experience and work record that should count, not paper qualifications." Discuss.

BITS AND PIECES

Won't be able to

Can't changes to *won't be able to* in the future tense.

Example: I can't go today, and I won't be able to go tomorrow, either.

Use *won't be able to* to respond to the following sentences.

Example: I bought two tickets in the last row.
But we won't be able to see anything.

1. She lost her driver's license yesterday.
2. He broke his leg during the game last week.
3. I left all my books at school.
4. I think their telephone is broken.
5. I lost the theater tickets.
6. He left Mary's address at home.
7. Someone just sat on my glasses.
8. They can't find their passports anywhere.
9. Tom can't find the marriage license.
10. The last two pages of that book are missing.
11. My record player just broke.
12. It just started raining.
13. I can't find the Spanish phrase book.
14. Where are our keys?
15. My boss wants me to work late tonight.

15

PRESENTATION

RICH GIRL, POOR BOY

They asked him if he could support Melissa.

Howard Murphy, a poor, young engineering student, wants to marry Melissa Gotrich, a very rich, young New York socialite. Howard has come to meet Melissa's whole family, who all disapprove of the engagement. They are sitting in the living room, asking Howard about himself and his plans. Aunt Maud, the oldest and richest member of the family, is hard of hearing. Because of this, the other family members are relaying the conversation to her in a louder voice.

Take the parts of the characters in the illustration and carry on the conversation as it is relayed to Aunt Maud. Use the cues provided for the questions, and your own ideas for Howard's answers.

The family wants to know:

—if they have definitely decided to get married

—Howard's hobbies and special interests

—his father's line of business

—if he owns any shares in big companies

—how old he is

—where he was born

—how long he's been studying engineering

—when he will get his diploma

—what he is going to do after he graduates

—if he can support Melissa

—where his family lives

—if he's ever been to Europe

—if he will be able to afford a nice house after they get married

Example: AUNT SYLVIA: Have you and Melissa definitely decided to get married?
AUNT MAUD: What did she say?
UNCLE ALEX: She asked him if they had definitely decided to get married.
HOWARD: Yes. We're getting married in six months.
AUNT MAUD: I can't hear a word he says!
COUSIN RUPERT: He said they were getting married in six months.

EXPANSION

Read the following play, taking the parts of the characters.

Honest Dan—a less than honest real estate agent
Mr. Weevil—a gullible client
Mrs. Weevil—his wife
Billy Weevil—their son
Miss Lane—Honest Dan's secretary

Honest Dan's Real Estate Agency

The first day

HONEST DAN: I'm telling you folks, it's a fabulous country house. They don't build them like that any more. One of our most eminent presidents slept there once, you know.

MRS. WEEVIL: It certainly sounds impressive.

HONEST DAN: And it's comfortable too! There's hot and cold running water, and every room has a view.

BILLY WEEVIL: I like the country: Maybe I can have a dog. The city is so noisy and dirty.

MR. WEEVIL: How soon can we see it?

HONEST DAN: Tomorrow—but by then it will probably be sold. Hundreds of people are dying to buy it.

MRS. WEEVIL: Aw, come on, Harvey. Let's!

BILLY WEEVIL: Yeah, Dad!

HONEST DAN: Maybe I can help you folks make up your minds. Listen, do you want to live in peace and comfort for the rest of your lives?

ALL: Well, yes, we do.

HONEST DAN: This is the place for you, then! It may be a little hard to get to, but you won't be sorry, I promise you. Now, can you pay me only 4,000 dollars as a down payment?

MR. WEEVIL: Do you mean right now?

HONEST DAN: Let me tell you this, Mr. Weevil. Don't wait, or you'll be sorry. Pay me now before someone else gets the house. Your money will go far, believe me!

MRS. WEEVIL: I think we can manage it, Harvey.

BILLY WEEVIL: It might be too late by tomorrow, Dad.

MR. WEEVIL: Well, ok, I'll write you a check.

The next day

MRS. WEEVIL: (*to Miss Lane*) Where's that no-good boss of yours? You won't believe what he sold us yesterday! He said there was hot and cold running water. It was running all right! Through the living room!

BILLY WEEVIL: Yeah! And he told us that every room had a view! It's a view of the river on all four sides!

MR. WEEVIL: He told us that an eminent president had once slept there. Now we know he meant George Washington when he was crossing the Delaware!

MISS LANE: I'd like to help you, but . . .

MRS. WEEVIL: He said it might be hard to get to, but he didn't mention the fact that the place was a *lighthouse* and that we would have to row for three hours to reach it!

MISS LANE: I understand how upset you must be, but I'm afraid there's nothing I can do. You see . . .

MRS. WEEVIL: But you don't understand. When he asked us if we wanted to live in peace and comfort for the rest of our lives, we all said yes, and then he asked us if we could pay him 4,000 dollars.

MR. WEEVIL: He told us to pay him right then, and not to wait, or someone else would get the house first. He said that we wouldn't be sorry and that our money would go far.

BILLY WEEVIL: Yeah! That was the biggest lie of all—that our money would go far.

MISS LANE: Well, that wasn't a lie, I'm afraid. Your money went *very* far. Honest Dan ran away to Tahiti this morning with your money and the money of the twelve other people who bought that same place!

Relate the conversation between Honest Dan and the Weevils as presented in the first half of the play (*The first day*). Use reported speech.

Example: Dan told them it was a fabulous country house. He said they didn't build them like that any more.

GRAMMAR SUMMARY

REPORTED SPEECH

Rather than always quoting direct speech, we often relate a person's exact words indirectly. When the reporting verb is in the past tense, certain grammatical changes are necessary.

I. Reported Statements
   a. Verbs in the present tense change to the past tense.

Examples: "I really like reading mystery stories."
He said that he really liked reading mystery stories.

"Harry and Janet are good friends."
She told me that Harry and Janet were good friends.

   b. Verbs in the present perfect change to the past perfect.

Examples: "I've been waiting for the bus for an hour."
She said that she had been waiting for the bus for an hour.

"I haven't been to a party in ages."
He said he hadn't been to a party in ages.

   c. *Will* changes to *would.*

Examples: "I'll help you with your homework."
He said he would help me with my homework.

"My son won't do anything I tell him to."
She told me that her son wouldn't do anything she told him to.

   d. In theory, the simple past tense changes to the past perfect tense, but it is usually left unchanged, especially in spoken English.

Examples: "I didn't go to sleep until 3:00 a.m."
He said that he didn't go to sleep until 3:00 a.m.

"We all went to the movies on Thursday."
They told him that they all went to the movies on Thursday.

   e. *May* changes to *might,* and *can* changes to *could.*

Examples: "I may call you tonight, but I'm not sure."
She said that she might call me tonight, but she wasn't sure.

"She can't understand the lesson," the teacher said.
The teacher said that she couldn't understand the lesson.

II. Reported Questions
   a. In reported questions the interrogative auxiliary words *do, does,* and *did* are omitted. The word order is the same as for a statement.

Examples: "Where does Norma live?"
He asked me where Norma lived.

"Can you help me?"
She asked me if I could help her.

b. In reported questions the verb *be* is placed at the end of the sentence or at the end of the clause in which it appears.

Examples: "Where's the nearest subway station?"
She asked him where the nearest subway station was.

"Where were they when the accident happened?"
The police asked us where they were when the accident happened.

III. Reported Commands
a. Affirmative commands are reported by using command words such as *tell, order,* and *command,* and then the person spoken to followed by an infinitive.

Examples: "Give me all the keys."
He told us to give him all the keys.

"Sit down."
He ordered them to sit down.

b. Negative commands are formed by using a negative infinitive.

Examples: "Don't forget your wallet."
He told me not to forget my wallet.

"Don't touch that knife."
She told him not to touch that knife.

Notes

i. *That* may be used after the reporting verb, but it is often omitted.

Example: He told me (that) I was too sick to leave the house.

ii. One sentence in reported speech can be used to relate two (or more) sentences in direct speech.

Example: "What do you think you're doing? Give me the gun."
She asked him what he thought he was doing, and told him to give her the gun.

iii. Tell/Say/Ask
a. The simple past tense of the verb *tell* is used in reported speech either to relate a statement or to give an order.

Examples: "I'm sick." He told us (that) he was sick.

"Open the door!" She told him to open the door.

Told must always be followed by an indirect object.

b. The simple past tense of the verb *say* is also used in reported speech, but it can never be followed by an indirect object. *Say* can never be used for commands.

Examples: "I won't be late." He said (that) he wouldn't be late.

"Don't open the door." She told me (NOT *said me*) to open the door.

Said can never be followed by an indirect object.

c. The simple past tense of the verb *ask* is used in reported questions and may or may not be followed by an indirect object.

Example: "What time is it?" He asked (me) what time it was.

The indirect object is never preceded by the preposition *to*.

Fred asked her (NOT *to her*) a question.
She told him (NOT *to him*) the truth.

INTENSIVE PRACTICE

I. Change the following questions into reported speech. Remember to use the correct word order, and begin each sentence with "He/She asked me . . ."

Example: "Where's the nearest post office?" she asked.
She asked me where the nearest post office was.

1. "How old is your English teacher?" he asked.
2. "What's your brother's address?" she asked.
3. "How much are the brown leather boots?" she asked.
4. "What time is it?" he asked.
5. "What are your qualifications for the job?" he asked.
6. "How old are your children?" she asked.
7. "What's your phone number?" he asked.
8. "What time is the next train to Boston?" she asked.
9. "Where's our alarm clock?" he asked.
10. "Where are the other students?" she asked.

II. The following sentences in direct speech are composed of two parts. Change them to reported speech, using the example as a model.

Example: "I'm a language teacher, but I've never taught French before."

She said (that) she was a language teacher, but that she had never taught French before.

1. "I'm going to the post office, but I'll be back in a few minutes."
2. "I've been working hard, and I'm ready for a vacation!"
3. "I was born in Canada, but I haven't lived there for years."
4. "I don't really understand what your problem is, but I'll try to help you anyway."
5. "I usually sleep about eight hours every night, but I still feel tired when I get up in the morning."

III. Change the following questions to reported speech. Make sure to leave out the auxiliary verb, and make all necessary changes in the other verbs.

Examples: "Do you always buy your clothes in that boutique?" she asked.

She asked me if I always bought my clothes in that boutique.

"What time did Carl and Bonnie get home?" he asked.

He asked me what time Carl and Bonnie got home.

1. "Where do you live?" he asked.
2. "Does the apartment have two bedrooms?" she asked.
3. "What time did the film begin?" he asked.
4. "Did a package come for me this morning?" she asked.
5. "Where did he go after he left the bank?" he asked.
6. "What did Sheila wear to the party?" she asked.
7. "How many children do you have?" he asked.
8. "Do you often drive to the beach on the weekends?" he asked.
9. "How much money did Bill win at the casino?" she asked.
10. "Does Peter always get up so late?" she asked.

IV. Change the following to reported speech. Use the examples as models.

Examples: "The radio is too loud! Turn it down!"
She said (that) _____ and told me _____ .
She said that the radio was too loud and told me to turn it down.

"I don't want to be late for work. Will you call me a taxi?"
He said (that) _____ and asked me if _____ .
He said that he didn't want to be late for work and asked me if I would call him a taxi.

1. "I can hear the police coming! Hide the money!"
   He said (that) _____ and told me _____ .
2. "I don't know where the children are. Do you?"
   She said (that) _____ and asked me if _____ .
3. "I'll give you twenty dollars. Don't spend it all!"
   She said (that) _____ and told me _____ .
4. "Mrs. Jones isn't at home. Can you call a little later?"
   She said (that) _____ and asked me if _____ .
5. "I've been waiting for two hours. Will you get me a cup of coffee?"
   He said (that) _____ and asked me if _____ .

V. You have received the following letter. You are telling a friend of yours about what was in the letter. Convey this information using reported speech.

Example: How are you?

First, she asked me how I was, and then she told me to prepare myself for some great news. She said . . .

Dear Robin,

How are you? Prepare yourself—I have some great news for you— I'm married! Do you remember Ralph N'koma? He's the guy I met in my English class. Well, we went to City Hall and took out our license. Nobody knows about it, so don't tell Sarah. I'll tell her myself next week.

I may arrive in Midville sometime next week, but I haven't made up my mind yet. I can't wait to see you! Sorry for not writing until now, but I've been very busy.

Love,
Sohaila

WRITING AND HOMEWORK

I. Turn the following into reported speech.

Example: Bill (*to Martha*): "Where's the nearest post office?"
He asked her where the nearest post office was.

1. Jim (*to his friends*): "What's Barbara's phone number?"
2. Mary (*to Susan*): "I'll be back in a few minutes."
3. Harry (*to his parents*): "Why can't I use the car?"
4. Judy (*to me*): "Do you have enough money?"
5. Carl (*to Jim*): "How old is Martha's sister?"
6. David's mother (*to David*): "Don't open the window!"
7. Mr. Henderson (*to his boss*): "When are you going to give me a raise?"
8. Mr. Benson (*to his wife*): "I haven't gone dancing in years!"
9. Bank robber (*to clerk*): "Give me all the money!"
10. Bob (*to Sarah*): "I can't find my new shirt!"

II. The following is a copy of Mayor Buster Biggs's speech at the opening of the new Midville hospital. You are a journalist for the Midville *Sun*, and your job is to write an article summarizing Mayor Biggs's speech. Write the article as it would appear in the newspaper, using reported speech when possible.

Midvillagers:

This is a proud day for Midville! The hospital we have all been waiting for is finally finished, and it only cost the taxpayers a million dollars! This new modern building has a main pavilion and an annex that will accommodate two hundred patients. The emergency ward has been equipped with a special burn center and fracture unit. There is also a telephone hot-line service which people can call any hour of the night or day. In the future this service may be expanded to include a poison information department.

Midville mayors have been promising to build a hospital ever since we can remember. Don't forget that it was Buster Biggs who kept his promise. Vote for me on November 5th!

Begin your article like this:

> **MAYOR BIGGS CUTS RIBBON**
> Mayor Buster Biggs proudly inaugurated Midville's first hospital today. In his speech, Mayor Biggs stated that it was a great day for Midville. He proudly informed the crowd that the hospital Midville had been waiting for was finally finished . . .

III. Listen carefully to a news item on the radio or TV and summarize the information, using reported speech when possible.

DISCUSSION

I. Take the parts of the people involved in each role play. After characters (a) and (b) have finished their dialogue, character (c) should try to relay what has been said in reported speech when possible.

THE RESTAURANT

a. You are in a restaurant. You see Linda Lane, a famous actress you have admired for years. Go over to her table and insist on getting her autograph.

b. You are Linda Lane. This person has interrupted an intimate dinner with a friend. You are extremely annoyed and refuse to give him(her) your autograph.

c. You are sitting at the next table. You describe the scene to your wife, who was in the ladies' room at the time.

THE ROBBERY

a. You are a bank robber and you are trying to convince your accomplice to rob the First National Bank in the middle of the day using a plastic pistol.

b. You are his partner. You disagree with his scheme and try to change his mind.

c. You have overheard the conversation between the two bank robbers and are trying to tell the police what they said.

THE PLANE TRIP

a. You are on a plane to Rio de Janeiro that is going to land in São Paulo because of bad weather. You are a very important person and must be in Rio by tonight. You are upset and insist that the plane land in Rio as scheduled.

b. You are a flight attendant. This person's unreasonable demands are making you lose your patience.

c. You are another flight attendant. You are telling the captain about the scene that has taken place.

THE DINNER

a. You have taken a party of twelve important company presidents to an exotic restaurant for a business dinner. The food tastes awful. You complain to the waiter.

b. You are the waiter. This man doesn't know anything about exotic food. You patiently explain that the food is supposed to taste that way.

c. You are the headwaiter of the restaurant. You are on the phone to the restaurant's manager, telling him about the incident.

THE SHOPLIFTING

a. You are a salesperson and you have caught someone shoplifting. You insist on calling the police.

b. You were intending to pay for the pair of socks, but you absent-mindedly put them in your pocket. You are shocked that the salesperson thinks you stole them, as you are an honest person and have never stolen anything in your life.

c. You are the manager of the store and are telling the store's owner the details of the incident.

II. Interview one of your classmates (or a native English speaker outside the class) on one of the following subjects. Report your findings to the class.

1. Automobile traffic should be prohibited in the city.
2. Families should be forced to take care of their elderly relatives.
3. There should be more women on the police force.
4. All high school students should be forced to study a second language.
5. Second marriages often work out better than first marriages.
6. Aspirin should only be sold with a medical prescription.
7. TV commercials serve a useful purpose.
8. Cigarettes should not be sold to minors.
9. Companies should give at least a month's vacation each year to their employees.
10. There will be no need for classroom teachers in the future.
11. TV should be more educational than recreational.
12. Marriage partners should be as much alike as possible.

BITS AND PIECES

Embedded Questions

Mr. Mot, a foreign tourist visiting the U.S., has gone to see the Tomb of the Unknown Soldier in Arlington, Virginia. There are a lot of questions he wants to ask the soldier guarding the tomb:

"Do many foreign tourists visit Arlington?"
"How long have you been an honor guard?"
"Is Washington, D.C., far from here?"
"How long does it take to get there by bus?"
"Will the Washington Monument be open this afternoon?"
"Are there any tourist shops in downtown Washington?"
"Can I exchange foreign money at any Washington bank?"
"Does the Lincoln Memorial stay open at night?"
"Do they sell maps of downtown Washington here in Arlington?"

I. Mr. Mot is thinking aloud. Beginning with *I wonder,* use the questions above and say what Mr. Mot is thinking.

Example: "Do many foreign tourists visit Arlington?"
"I wonder if many foreign tourists visit Arlington."

II. Dying of curiosity, Mr. Mot decides to question the honor guard. He inquires politely:

Example: Could you tell me | if many foreign tourists visit Arlington?
Would you mind telling me |

Continue Mr. Mot's questions, using the cues above.

Fifteen minutes later, terribly discouraged, Mr. Mot is talking to the honor guard who still hasn't answered any of his questions. "These Americans certainly aren't very polite," he says to himself. "I've certainly been polite in my questions. It's probably my English. I don't understand it. I've studied from *Gallery* for such a long time. I thought I'd learned a lot."

"What's the matter, Mister? Anything wrong?" Mot hears the pleasant voice of the man standing behind him.

"Yes. I'm so discouraged. It's my English. That guard doesn't understand a word I say. He won't answer me."

"He won't even answer the President. Honor guards are not supposed to speak to anyone. Don't worry. Your English is great!"

TEACHER'S NOTES

1 I READ IT IN THE NEWSPAPER

Presentation
Students read the first article silently.

Teacher introduces new vocabulary.

Teacher calls on individuals to retell the story as shown in activity 2.

Teacher chooses one or more students to take the role(s) of the person(s) being interviewed in activity 3. The rest of the class asks them questions using the question words supplied.

Same procedure as described above is followed for the other three articles.

Variations

i. With the students' books closed, the teacher reads each article first, and then follows procedures 2 and 3.

ii. Activity 3 may be done with students divided into pairs. Each pair is given a different article. One student takes the role of the interviewee, and the other, the reporter. After the interviews have been conducted, the teacher chooses several pairs to model the questions and answers for the whole class.

Expansion

1. Students read "Mystery Story" silently, or teacher reads it for listening comprehension.

   Teacher introduces new vocabulary.

   With books closed, students ask and answer questions using the question words in activity 1. Teacher may write question words on the blackboard as a reminder of the question forms being practiced.

2. Teacher conducts an informal class discussion, noting student errors. Predominant errors can be brought to the students' attention afterwards.

Variations

i. For further practice, students can narrate the whole story as the teacher mimes the main actions.

ii. Tic Tac Toe: The teacher makes a large tic tac toe grid on the blackboard and fills in each space with one of the question words or phrases.

WHERE	WHO	WHEN
WHAT	HOW	WHAT KIND
WHAT TIME	WHY	WHOSE

The class is divided into two teams. Each team takes turns asking a question using one of the words or phrases in the tic tac toe grid. Questions should be based on the story. The teacher marks off each completed, correct question on the grid, using X's for one team and 0's for the other. The team that first makes a straight line (across, down, or diagonal) wins the game.

Intensive Practice

I. Teacher explains that the first clause is in the affirmative and the second clause in the negative.

A student models the sample item.

Individual students are called on to complete each item, using the verb indicated.

In this drill, as in many others in the Intensive Practice sections, the teacher may choose to animate the exercise by putting the cues on flashcards.

Example:

(call)
fire department/ambulance

(enjoy)
book/film

II. The teacher follows the same procedure as described for exercise I. As with the preceding exercise, the cues can also be put on flashcards.

III. The teacher calls on two students to read A and B of the example.

New sets of students are then chosen to do items 1–5.

IV. The teacher explains that speaker B will have to provide an original sentence to conclude the short dialogues in the exercise.

Two students are chosen to read the model 4-line dialogue.

Other student pairs are selected to do 4-line dialogues for items 1–10.

V. Teacher chooses two students to read the sample dialogue.

Other student pairs do items 1–5.

The teacher may want to have the students extend the dialogues beyond three lines.

Example: A: Guess what my brother did the other day?
B: I don't know. What did he do?
A: He forgot his wife's birthday.
B: How did his wife feel about that?
A: Well, she got mad, left the house, and went to a nice restaurant by herself.

Writing and Homework

I. The students are instructed to fill in the blank spaces with an appropriate verb in the past tense.

II. Using the page out of the diary as a reference, the students write an account of Hans Schmidt's day in paragraph form. The students can be encouraged to add original information.

Example: Hans Schmidt, the Foreign Minister of Lebensraum, arrived in Washington yesterday. He checked in at the Hotel Columbia at 10:45, went up to his room, took a shower, and left the hotel.

III. Using the short newspaper article as a reference, the student should write an original story, this time with Jack Wilkins as the protagonist. The first half of the students' stories will remain essentially the same regarding content. It is in the second half that the students will have to use their imaginations by providing an account of Jack's past life. One possibility would be: . . . That evening Jack's wife hypnotized him. When she asked how he felt, Jack opened his eyes, jumped out of the bed, and shouted, "Where is my sword?" After Mrs. Wilkins had calmed her husband down, he started to describe the details of his past life as a pirate. . . .

Discussion

I. The teacher may want to assign one item to the whole class or divide the five themes among all the class members, giving item 1 to a few students, item 2 to another few students, etc. In any case, it would be best to assign the topics from one class period to the next, since students often find it difficult to come up with stories on short notice.

Each student is called on to tell his narrative to the whole class; the teacher notes down any grammar errors made and discusses them with the class afterwards.

In the cases of items 2, 3, and 5, other class members can be encouraged to ask the narrator pertinent questions after the story has been told.

The students can be paired off. Each pair partner tells his narrative to the other. Class members are then responsible for telling the whole class the story each heard.

II. The students are instructed to find and read an interesting newspaper article in English or another language they are acquainted with. During the next class period, students are called on to come to the front of the room and recount the details of the article. The teacher takes notes of errors and discusses them afterwards.

Variations

i. The students can be required to recount the contents of the article they read as if they were speaking on a TV news program.

Example: "Good evening, ladies and gentlemen. I'm Frank Harper, and this is the seven o'clock news. Today in Midville, police were called to the home of Mr. John Brown. . . ."

ii. The teacher informs the class that a good newspaper article should always provide the answers to the major *who, what, why, where, when,* and *how* questions. After each student has recounted his article, the teacher asks the students if all the important information has been given. Students think of all the information gaps in the student's narrative and try to fill them by asking the narrator questions.

Example: "You didn't tell us *why* the man took the money" or
"But, *why* did the man take the money?" or
"How did he break into the bank? You didn't say."

Bits and Pieces

I. Individual students are asked to combine sentences 1–5 orally using "even though" (see example).

II. Individual students are asked to combine sentences 1–5 orally, using "even though" and "managed to" (see example).

III. Teacher asks students to read the paragraph silently.

Teacher introduces new vocabulary.

Teacher calls on individual students to create sentences from the text with "even though" and "managed to" (see example).

2 PANIC AT THE AVON HOTEL

Presentation

I. Students are told to look at the pictures. They then take turns asking and answering questions about the pictures in the present continuous tense.

Example: s1: What is Mr. Lockhart doing in this picture?
s2: He's reading the newspaper.

This way, the teacher checks the students' knowledge of the vocabulary needed. The teacher should provide the verb if the student is not able to.

The teacher calls the students' attention to the vocabulary items in I and explains any new words.

The teacher emphasizes that the picture shows a cross-section of the hotel a minute before the explosion and asks a student:
T: What was Mr Lockhart doing when the bomb exploded?
S: He was reading the newspaper (when the bomb exploded).

After modeling the question/answer technique, the teacher has student pairs continue the procedure, using the visual cues and any of the word cues provided.

Examples: s1: What were Mr. and Mrs. Snodgrass doing when the walls crumbled?
s2: They were putting together an old vase (when the walls crumbled).
s3: What was Camomilla Voceforte doing when the building shook?
s4: When the building started shaking, she was rehearsing for a performance (or singing).

II. This activity is done as a roleplay. One student is chosen to be a reporter and another, one of the characters in the pictures. The interview is conducted as shown in the example. The teacher should instruct the students to use the past continuous in the first two lines, and the past simple tense (in contrast) in the following lines. The students are responsible for providing original information in the last lines of the dialogue.

Expansion

Students are instructed to read the text silently.

Teacher introduces new vocabulary.

Students read the text again silently.

Teacher reads the example (He was reading the newspaper when the doorbell rang), then the contradiction (*That's* not right . . .), taking care to stress the word "that's."

The teacher then reads items 1–10, calling on individual students to correct the statements.

Variations

With the aid of simple drawings and cues on the blackboard, the teacher can use mime to elicit the events in the story.

Intensive Practice

I. Students are asked to combine the two sets of cues, first using "while" and then "when" (see example). Two different students should be called on for each item.

II. Two questions are to be formed from the cues provided. The first question is in the negative-interrogative of the past tense, the second question in the past continuous.

These cues may also be transferred onto flashcards.

III. The teacher calls the students' attention to the intonation pattern in B. Individual students can be called on to read B of the example or the teacher may choose to chorally drill the class.

A student pair is then chosen to do the sample dialogue.

Students are then told that they will have to provide the information for the last half of the last speech.

Student pairs are then chosen to do items 1–10.

IV. This exercise is also done in dialogue form. In numbers 1–6 the first half is in the interrogative. In items 7–10, the first half is in the negative-interrogative. Using the cues, S1 forms a question to which S2 responds in the past continuous tense, also using the cues provided.

V. In this exercise students practice the contrast between the past continuous and the past tense. The first two lines of the dialogue involve a question and a corresponding answer in the past continuous tense. The next two lines are a question and corresponding answer in the past simple tense. Students are to use the cues provided to complete the dialogue.

VI. The teacher should read the example, showing the students how they must stress the italicized words.

The teacher then calls on individual students to do items 1–10.

Writing and Homework

I. The teacher explains that a "come as you are" party is one in which the guests have to come exactly as they were when they received the invitation phone call. By looking at the description of each guest, students have to list what they think that guest was doing when he (or she) received the call.

Examples: 1. Mary was cooking dinner when Linda phoned.
2. Jim was getting ready for bed (or sleeping) when Linda called.

II. In this guided composition, students are to make complete sentences from the cues given.

Example: I was sitting in the backyard, reading the newspaper, when suddenly the sky got dark. It was really frightening! . . . etc.

The teacher may want to have the students say the dialogue in class after it has been written out.

III. In this exercise, students are required to write an original interview-type dialogue. They may refer to the preceding exercise for general ideas. It will not be possible, however, to use exercise II as a real guide, since the incidents differ too greatly.

Discussion

I. The teacher asks a student to read each quote. A discussion of the implications of the quote follows with the teacher eliciting opinions from class members. Mistakes are written down by the teacher as they occur, and discussed afterward.

II. The teacher follows the same procedure as described in I.

Bits and Pieces

I. The teacher explains that both "would you like me to" and "should I" are employed here as offers of help.

Individual students are called on to do items 1–10 orally, as shown in the example. Each item requires two sentences, to be done by two different students.

II. Either the teacher or a student reads the introduction to the exercise.

The class discusses the motivation behind Philip's politeness.

Pairs are chosen to model the procedure.

New Aunt Agatha–Philip pairs are selected to do mini-dialogues based on the cues given. Students should be encouraged to "elaborate" and inject a note of theatrics in their exchanges.

Example:
AUNT AGATHA: Philip! Philip!
PHILIP: What is it Aunt Agatha? I'm right here!
A: I don't feel well. I have a terrible headache and my feet are killing me.
P: Poor Auntie! Should I get you an aspirin?
A: I can't take aspirins. You know that!
P: Would you like me to get you a cold towel to put on your head? And should I bring you a basin of hot water to put your feet in?
A: What a horrible idea! . . .

3   FAMILY ALBUM

Presentation

Teacher points out that the illustration shows a page from a family album, and goes over the characteristics (superstitious, absent-minded, etc.) of each of the six relatives, answering questions about new vocabulary.

Teacher explains that John, Mary, Pamela, and Michael are reminiscing about their relatives. Students then read the model dialogue for comprehension.

At this point the teacher can explain that the actions in the conversation are habitual, past actions, and that to indicate these kinds of past actions, we use *would, was always . . .ing,* and *used to.*

Cues for Cousin Sarah are then put on the blackboard, and the teacher elicits three statements about her past actions with *would, was always . . .ing,* and *used to* respectively.

Examples:

Cues (on blackboard)	Student responses
a rabbit's foot	"She would always have/carry a rabbit's foot with her."
knock on wood	"She was always knocking on wood."
her horoscope	"She used to read her horoscope (every day/all the time)."

I. Students then incorporate these statements into a conversation as shown in the model, taking the parts of the four family members. Teacher can point out such conversational elements as "Look at this picture" and "How could I ever forget!" beforehand.

II. Teacher then elicits statements about the other relatives using *would (always),* *was always . . .ing,* and *used to* as previously done with Cousin Sarah. The blackboard can be used again, or students can simply refer to the cues beside each relative's picture.

When students can manipulate these basic elements, they can be asked to take the parts of the four characters as they talk about their relatives (as previously done for Cousin Sarah).

Variations

After students have practiced sentences about Cousin Sarah, using *would, was always . . .ing,* and *used to* as shown in I, the teacher can continue eliciting similar sentences about the other relatives, instead of practicing the conversation right away.

When students can manipulate these sentences, they can be divided into groups of four and instructed to take the parts of John, Mary, Pamela, and Michael.

Each group talks about a different relative and practices short conversations similar to the model.

When they are able to go through the conversation without referring to the text (or referring only to the cues beside the pictures), the groups of four can perform the conversations for the rest of the class.

Expansion

Students read text silently, and teacher answers questions about vocabulary.

Teacher checks for general comprehension by helping students retell the story.

Example: | Teacher asks: | "How can you tell from the story that Horace was really proud of his cousin Mike?"

Cues for student responses (oral or written on blackboard): —pictures out of movie magazines
—Mike's face—posters and billboards

Teacher asks: "What about their experiences at school?"

Cues: —in the school yard together
—into trouble
—apples from the corner grocery store
—classes

Teacher asks: "What did Horace read in the newspaper one day?" and "What did Horace say to the reporters?"

Note: At this point the teacher is only checking for comprehension, so she should not insist that students answer the questions using the structure (*would, was always . . .ing,* and *used to*).

Activity: Teacher goes over the example with students and then chooses individuals to ask questions in turn as cued in the exercise. Other students are chosen to answer the questions.

Example: STUDENT 1: Who was always slamming the kitchen door?
STUDENT 2: Horace's wife was.

The questions and answers may be assigned as in-class writing assignments or given as homework.

Variations

With students' books closed, the text can be read twice, at normal speed, by the teacher, as a listening comprehension exercise.

To check for comprehension, teachers can ask questions similar to the ones above.

The cues on the left of the activity can be written on flashcards. Teacher then writes *would (always), was always . . .ing,* and *used to* on the blackboard and elicits "who" questions by showing a flashcard and pointing to the appropriate key word(s) on the board. Other students answer the questions.

Intensive Practice

   I. Teacher first elicits *used to* sentences for all 12 items. The exercise is then done again, first with *would always,* and once more with *was always . . .ing.*

  II. After going over the example with students, teacher elicits questions with *used to* in the negative-interrogative. Teacher should first model the intonation. Cues can also be written on flashcards.

 III. This drill should be done first with *was always . . .ing* and then again with *would always.* When the students have practiced the exercise with both expressions, teacher can do the drill again using board cues or word flashcards, this time omitting the verb, which students will have to supply.

 IV. Teacher familiarizes students with the procedure by going over both examples. Then individual students can be called upon to do the exercise. If the length of each item is unwieldy for students at first, they can practice the first part of each item before adding the second sentence.

  V. Students are told that they are reminiscing about an imaginary rich uncle (who is also a bit weird). After going over the instructions and example, teacher calls on individual students to do the exercise using *would always.*

Writing and Homework

   I. Part 1 (1–5) Students fill in the blanks using *used to* and a logical verb.

     Part 2 (1–5) Students fill in the blanks of this second group of sentences with *was/were always . . .ing* or *would always* and an appropriate verb.

  II. Students are told that many verbs are missing from the story. Some of these verbs will be put in the past simple tense. Others, however, that indicate a past routine or a prolonged state in the past will be accompanied by *would, was always . . .ing,* or *used to.*

     Students will have to supply a logical verb and by referring to the small letters in the text and the key at the end of the story, they will know whether to use (a) *used to,* (b) *was/were always,* (c) *would,* or (d) *past tense.*

 III. This exercise will show if students understand the distinctions between the three forms. Students choose one of the topics and write a composition of approximately 100 words.

     The teacher can underline composition errors without correcting them, and ask students to try and correct their own mistakes. Teacher can go over common errors and those involving the structure (*would, was always . . .ing,* and *used to*) on the blackboard for the benefit of all the students.

Discussion

   I. Students should be given time to prepare this exercise in case they decide to consult an encyclopedia or other source, although they may draw on their own general knowledge if they wish. Topics should be divided evenly among students, the teacher taking into account individual preferences.

On the day of the discussion, students with the same topics give their talks one after the other so that they can complement each other' findings. The teacher encourages general class discussion of each topic.

II. Teacher reads the three examples of what people used to believe and gives students a few minutes to think of some things they (or people they know) used to believe. Pairs of students exchange stories of what they used to believe. Each student then tells the class not about his own experience, but about that of his partner.

Bits and Pieces

I. After going over the instructions and example with students, teacher calls on individuals to change the exercise items using *whenever, whatever,* or *wherever.*

II. Students read the story *Monkey Business* silently. Teacher then goes over vocabulary.

Teacher explains that students have to make statements about Rupert and Corky with *whenever, wherever,* or *whatever.*

Teacher may write the following cues from the first two paragraphs of the text on the blackboard, eliciting a *whenever, wherever,* or *whatever* sentence for each one.

Examples: Wherever Rupert sat, Corky would always sit too.
Whenever Rupert watched TV, Corky would do the same.
Whenever Rupert sang, Corky would sing too.

Cues: Rupert	*Corky*
sat somewhere	sat there too
watched TV	did the same
sang	sang too
ate something	pretended to do the same
lit a cigarette	imitated him
went somewhere	followed him
made abstract drawings	imitated him
dialed a number on the phone	did the same on the extension
felt sad	seemed to suffer too

Teacher then writes cues on the board in the present tense from paragraph three of the text, eliciting statements as before. This time, students take the part of Rupert as he talks to his friend about Corky.

Examples: Whenever I pick up a book, he does the same.
Whenever I turn on the radio in the living room, he turns on the one in the kitchen.

Cues: I	*he*
pick up a book	picks one up too
turn on the radio in the living room	turns on the one in the kitchen
laugh	laughs
smile	smiles
hide my money	hides his cookies there
light a cigarette	pretends to do the same.

4   THE CARDIGANS' DAY IN COURT

Presentation

I. Students read the text silently.

Teacher explains vocabulary items students might not have understood.

Teacher calls on individual students to ask questions based on the italicized words and phrases (see example).

Teacher calls on other individual class members to answer the questions.

II. Teacher assigns the role of Mrs. Cardigan to one of the students. Another student takes the part of her lawyer. The two students model the sample dialogue.

The students are encouraged to use the words *make, let, force, oblige, order,* and *want* in their questions and answers. The teacher can write these key words on the blackboard as a reminder and point to specific words to be used as the dialogue is being performed.

Two other students are chosen for the roles of Mrs. Cardigan and her lawyer. Using the key words, the two students perform the dialogue, with Mrs. Cardigan answering according to two of the cues in her dialogue bubble.

Two more lawyer–Mrs. Cardigan pairs are chosen, and the same procedure is followed.

The teacher then chooses a lawyer–Mr. Cardigan pair to model a dialogue.

The same procedure as described above is followed until all of Mr. Cardigan's cues have been used.

Variations

i. The students can feel free to change the wording in the sample dialogue. Variations in certain phrases and additional comments by the students are welcome, as long as the structure focused is practiced.

ii. After the courtroom dialogues are finished, students can be encouraged to ask and answer questions about what was said.

Examples: S1: What did Mr. Cardigan want his wife to do?
S2: He wanted her to cook gourmet meals every day.
S3: What did Mrs. Cardigan make her husband do?
S4: She made him help with the dishes.

iii. Another courtroom scene can be set up in which, this time, students have to come up with different accusations.

iv. A free class discussion can follow in which students tell about real-life cases of incompatibility and/or situations that led to divorce.

Expansion

Without assigning roles, the teacher asks the students to read the play silently. New vocabulary is discussed and explained.

The teacher or individual students ask class members information questions regarding the text.

Example: TEACHER OR S1: What did the hijacker warn the passengers not to do?
S2: He warned them not to scream.

The teacher asks each student if there is a specific charcter he would like to play. Roles are assigned according to student preferences.

If there are more class members than parts, the students left over are assigned understudy roles.

If the class is large enough, the play can be done by two groups.

Students then sit in a circle. Each character in turn looks down at his lines, then looks up and says as much of it as he can remember, while looking at the person he is supposed to be talking to. Students should never deliver their lines while looking at the script. If the student cannot remember a whole line of dialogue, he should pause, look down again, then look up again and deliver the rest. Students should *all* be looking up, not down at the play, when a line is being delivered.

At first, delivery of lines is very halting, but with the technique described above, dialogue memorization becomes easier, and the reading of lines is minimized.

When students are able to go through the play without referring to their lines, the teacher then discusses with them how the staging and direction of characters should be handled.

Classroom props are chosen, the scene is set, and students perform the play.

Variations

i. If recording equipment is available, a tape can be made of the performance of the play. Students and teachers discuss the effectiveness of the delivery and points of pronunciation and intonation after hearing the tape.

ii. If there is not enough time available to do the play as an actual classroom drama exercise, the teacher can have students read the play as described above, but eliminate the performance component.

Intensive Practice

I. In each one of the ten items, the teacher calls on one class member to formulate the question half of the item, and another student to do the answer component. (see example)

II. Individual students are asked to form a question based on the italicized information. Questions will use either the verb *want* (see example) or the expression *would like* (numbers 1, 4, 7, and 9).

III. Teacher explains that students are to transform the exercise items, using *make* and *let* as shown in the examples. Teacher then calls on individual students to do the sample sentences. Students then transform items 1 to 15 using "When I was a child, my parents let me/didn't let me; made me/didn't make me. . ." accordingly.

IV. Teacher explains procedure to students, and then individual students make "want to do" questions based on each item. Another student answers the question logically. Two students model sample sentences. Pairs of students are then called on to do items 1 to 10.

V. Students are told they have to combine the cues in the first column with the quotes in the second column. They are also reminded that object pronouns must be used and that other pronoun changes will take place. Individual students are called on to do the example. Individual class members then do items 1–10.

Writing and Homework

I. Students are told that they must rewrite Ken's speech, inserting the words *make, let, allow, permit, force, oblige,* and *warn* when possible. The example shows how the key words can be fit into the text.

II. The students are told to refer to the text in the **Presentation** for ideas. They will, however, have to provide ideas of their own. Tell the students to imagine the type of dialogue that would take place between two close friends. Joan's lines should include the words called for in the instructions.

Example: JOAN: I'm so unhappy. My parents were right. You know they didn't want me to marry Vince. My mother begged me to change my mind.
FRIEND: I didn't know that. I thought they agreed to the marriage.
JOAN: No, my father especially wanted me to finish college. . . .

III. Students are asked to remember frustrating experiences they have had involving bureaucracy. The teacher may discuss an individual student's experiences in class to illustrate how *told, ask, want,* and *make* can be used to describe these circumstances. The students must then write a descriptive paragraph using the above words whenever possible.

Example: Last September I decided to get married. I thought it would be easy, but they made me give them my birth certificate and then they told me to get a blood test. When I thought I'd gotten everything together, they then told me to bring them my fiancé's birth certificate. . . .

The students can be encouraged to invent details to make their stories funnier and more frustrating.

Discussion

I. The class is divided into two opposing groups which get together to plan a strategy. Each group will have to think of comments and facts detrimental to the opposing side. If the enactment of the court case is assigned for another day, students can arrange to bring to class such extras as "incriminating" letters, movie tickets, etc.

A judge is chosen, and each group member is called on to give his (or her) damaging testimony.

The judge, basing his decision on the effectiveness of the group's collective performance, decides who is to have custody of the child.

The teacher should take note of any major grammar errors she hears, and discuss them with the class afterwards.

II. Two students are chosen to do the first roleplay.

The pair reads the situation and then goes up to the front of the room to enact it.

The teacher must be careful not to let the situation run on too long.

The teacher takes notes of major grammar errors as they occur.

When the students have sat down, the class discusses the effectiveness of the scene. Was it true to life? Would everyone in the class have handled the situation the same way?

The teacher then selects students to do the other roleplays, following the procedure described above.

Bits and Pieces

I. Students are told that *will* is often used as an offer of help.

A student is called on to read the first item. Another class member must provide an appropriate offer of help with "I'll . . ."

Remaining items are done with the teacher following the procedure described above.

II. 1. Students are told that *won't* (for the present) and *wouldn't* (for the past) are often used to express refusal.

One student is assigned the part of Mrs. Norton and another student the neighbor. The two students read the model dialogue.

The teacher calls on two new students to create a similar dialogue based on the next cue.

Other student pairs are chosen to do the rest of the items, until all of the cues have been used.

2. Using the same cues as in exercise 1, individual students take the parts of Mrs. Norton and the neighbor and deliver the dialogues, this time in the simple past tense.

Example: MRS. NORTON: I kept telling him to clean his room, but he simply refused.
NEIGHBOR: You mean he wouldn't clean up his room when you told him to?
MRS. NORTON: That's right. He wouldn't do *anything* I told him to.

3. Using *won't* to indicate refusal in the present, students are called on to complete the sentences orally.

4. Using *wouldn't* to indicate refusal in the past, individual students are called on to complete the sentences orally.

5   BREAK-IN AT THE DUBCEKS'

Presentation

Students read the paragraph at the beginning of this section and the cues beside the picture. Teacher goes over vocabulary problems and then asks the students comprehension questions about the robbery.

Examples: What was in Judge Dubcek's safe?
Why was there a guard outside his home?
What happened one day when the Dubcek family was out?
What did they do to the guard?
What about the alarm system?

I. Teacher goes over instructions above the first dialogue, which students then read silently for comprehension.

At this point the teacher should explain to students that *had* + the past participle indicates an action that occurred before another past action.

Teacher then elicits short dialogues using the cues beside the illustration as the students take the parts of the judge and his wife.

II. Teacher then elicits similar short dialogues, this time in the passive as shown in the example.

Variations

Before practicing the dialogues in I and II, teacher can write the cues on the blackboard and elicit a statement for each one beginning, "By the time the Dubceks got home . . .". Students continue the sentence using the cues and *already* + the present perfect.

Example: Cue: knocked out the guard
            STUDENT: By the time the Dubceks got home, the criminals had already knocked out the guard.

When statements have been made about all the cues, the teacher erases the verbs and students are called upon to make statements again, this time supplying the verb themselves.

Example: Cue: the guard
            STUDENT: By the time the Dubceks got home, the criminals had already knocked out/tied up and gagged the guard.

Students can then be asked to make statements from the cues a third time, this time using pronouns to replace the people (or animals) in the cues.

Example: Cue: the guard
            STUDENT: By the time the Dubceks got home, the criminals had already knocked him out/tied him up and gagged him.

Expansion

Students read the story "Faulks' Inn" silently for comprehension. Then the teacher and students discuss any unknown vocabulary.

Teacher can check for comprehension by asking such general questions as: Who was Julie Faulks? Why did Connell decide to spend a night in the room?

I. Students then break into groups of five and divide the parts among themselves. If one of the groups has fewer than five members, students can double up on some of the parts (e.g. the innkeeper and the guest can be played by the same person).

Teacher tells groups that they are going to perform a radio drama, and that such things as proper intonation and expression are essential. Students practice the story several times with the teacher monitoring their efforts and offering suggestions.

If taping equipment is available, each group should record the story. Different versions can then be compared.

II. This activity can take several class hours to carry out, but it provides creative and highly motivated students with an interesting project. One or more groups of students are told to adapt "Faulks' Inn" to be performed as a short play for the rest of the class or an even larger student audience. The number of characters may have to be increased to suit the number of players.

Intensive Practice

I. Teacher may write the cues shown in the example on the blackboard and model the response, showing students what is required. Individual students are then asked to do the ten items in the exercise.

II. Students transform the items in this exercise as shown in the example. Then with books closed, students can try to do the exercise again, this time from oral cues supplied by the teacher.

III. Students are told that they have to supply a logical verb for each item. Teacher can point out that the past perfect tense is used, since the action occurred before another past action. Students are then called upon to do each item in the exercise.

IV. After doing this exercise as shown in the example, students, with books closed, can try to give the responses again, this time from oral cues supplied by the teacher.

V. Teacher points out that many events of great importance took place before the year 1500 and goes through the ten items shown in the exercise with the students.

  A. Students are then asked to make sentences with "By the year____" + the past perfect and *already,* referring to each of the facts. The first two items have been done as examples.

  B. Following the same procedure as in A), students make sentences in the passive as shown in the examples.

Writing and Homework

  I. Students are instructed to fill in the blanks using the past perfect tense and the verb in parentheses.

 II. A. Students are reminded that this exercise is similar to the one they did orally—V of the Intensive Practice section. As shown in the example, students write statements using the past perfect and *already.*

  B. Students make statements in the passive for the same ten facts, as shown in the example.

III. Students choose one of the last lines shown and write a composition of approximately 100 words. The teacher can read especially well done compositions in class. The corrections techniques mentioned in the notes for Chapter 3 (**Writing and Homework,** exercise III) can be used.

Discussion

  I. The class can be divided into six or more pairs. Pair one is instructed to think of the advantages that a twentieth century "achievement," such as the invention of the automobile, has brought us. Other twentieth century "achievements" such as the computer, the airplane, nuclear power, etc., can be similarly assigned to other student pairs.

  After approximately fifteen minutes of discussion between pair-partners, students present their arguments for or against a given "achievement." Rival groups can attack each others' arguments.

  Teacher notes down errors to be dealt with later and decides the winners of the confrontations on the basis of the forcefulness of the arguments presented.

 II. The short quotation is meant to spark a conversation about supernatural experiences. Students can recount stories they have heard, or tell of inci-

dents they have actually experienced. The teacher can also ask students
what/if they know about: ghosts
telepathy
ouija boards
séances
déjà vu
psychokinesis
etc.

Bits and Pieces

Teacher goes over the explanation of *might as well* given in the text and models
the two examples.

Students then read the sample situation and one student is called upon to model
the statements that follow.

Teacher then calls on individuals to do the exercise items.

6 ASK THE EXPERTS

Presentation

Amy Post's Problem Corner

Teacher has one or two students read the letter aloud and checks for comprehension of vocabulary.

Teacher or individual students ask information questions to check comprehension of the text.

Examples: TEACHER (OR STUDENT): How did Herman eat his chicken?
STUDENT 2: (He ate it) with his fingers.
TEACHER (OR STUDENT): Where did he clean his hands?
STUDENT 2: (He cleaned them) on the tablecloth.

I. Students are told that they are to form "opinion" questions based on the
italicized information. The questions and answers will be formed with either
should or *ought to.*

Teachers whose target group are learners of American English should explain at this point that *ought to,* when not imbedded, can only be used in
the affirmative. Ought to, in American English, is often pronounced /ɔda/.

A pair of students is called on to read the example.

New pairs of students continue asking and answering questions about what
people (in general) *should/ought to* do. Students should be encouraged to
give their opinions freely.

Examples: STUDENT 1: Do you think people *should/ought to* drink soup from the bowl?
STUDENT 2: No, I don't think they should/ought to. People should always use a spoon.
I think drinking from the bowl is rude.
STUDENT 3: Should people drink Coca Cola or other soft drinks from the bottle?
STUDENT 4: I think they ought to drink out of a glass, except, for example, at picnics
when drinking from the bottle is all right.

II. The teacher asks the students if they think that formal manners are a thing
of the past.

Ask Doctor Walters

The teacher follows the same procedure as described above, omitting, of course, the grammar explanation.

   I. Students ask and answer questions about the man who is writing the letter and his wife.

Example:

STUDENT 1: Do you think this woman should/ought to work twelve hours a day?

STUDENT 2: Personally, I don't think anybody should/ought to work twelve hours a day, but sometimes it can't be avoided.

STUDENT 3: Should working women have to make dinner and clean the house if they have an outside job?

STUDENT 4: I think husbands ought to help their working wives or even do all the housework if the woman works longer hours outside the home.

   II. The teacher asks the students what they think "Desperate Husband" can do to help his wife.

Students give opinions with teacher correcting major grammar errors as they occur.

You and Your Child and *The Heart Line*

Teacher follows the same procedure as described for the other two letters.

Variations

  i The teacher assigns one (or more) letter(s) to each student in the class. The students are told to *write* a reply to the letter as if they were the columnist in question. This written exercise can be done as an in-class activity or homework assignment. This exercise is a good follow-up to the oral work previously outlined.

  ii The class is divided into four groups. Each group is assigned a different letter. The members of the group have to decide together what the *worst* possible advice for their letter would be. A group secretary takes notes which the group members can use later as a reminder. After the groups have gotten their ideas together, each group member takes turns presenting the group's bad advice to the whole class. The teacher should take notes on any major grammar errors that arise and discuss them afterwards.

  iii Students can be asked to find advice column letters in local newspapers. The next class period, each student will be responsible for orally paraphrasing the contents of the letter he found for the whole class. The letters must *not* be read. After the student finishes telling the rest of the class about the letter, class members should be encouraged to think of the best advice to give the author of the letter. Since students will be paraphrasing the contents of the letters in English, foreign language newspapers may be used. If so, students should be urged not to translate the letter, but to summarize its main ideas.

Expansion

  I. Since this exercise follows a panel discussion format, participating students should be seated in a circle if possible.

Students who cannot be included in the reading should also be included in the circle.

Teacher tells students that what they will read is a TV discussion with members of the police force.

Students read text silently and the teacher then explains vocabulary that was not understood.

Students are selected to read *TV Journal* aloud.

Teacher has students question each other on what people should do before going on vacation.

Example: STUDENT 1: What should people remember to do before they go on vacation?
STUDENT 2: Well, first they should take their cars to the garage for a safety check.
STUDENT 3: What else should vacationers remember to do?
STUDENT 4: They should cancel all deliveries to their homes.

The teacher can write a list of cues on the blackboard. Example: safety check, deliveries, neighbors, light, blinds, travelers' checks, baggage, etc.

The roles are then reassigned—this time to include any students who were previously left out. The role of Lefty Evans can be changed to that of another police officer who will this time give good advice. Students conduct the discussion again without referring to their textbooks and using the cues on the blackboard as a reference. Their informal discussion, it is obvious, does not in any way have to duplicate the text. Students should feel free to add or omit information if they wish. The main purpose of this exercise is for the students to use their own words to transmit the main ideas in the text.

II. The students are asked to imagine an odd situation in which a group of burglars might be interviewed on a TV talk show or radio program. Names such as Slippery Louie, Sam the Fox, Dangerous Doris, Lefty Evans, Terrible Ed, Chicago Charlie, etc., can be assigned to the participants.

One of the students or the teacher can take the role of the reporter who introduces the discussion that is to follow. The intro may run as follows:

Ladies and Gentlemen, tonight we have with us a group of burglars who will give some advice to people about to leave on vacation. Their advice is pretty sound— as long as you follow it *in reverse!* Slippery Louie, what are your suggestions to people who are going on vacation?

The student taking the part of Slippery Louie could say something like this:

STUDENT: Well, first, all vacationers ought to remember not to cancel any deliveries of milk, newspapers, or mail to their homes. They should always ask their neighbors not to bother to check their house while they are gone.

Students taking the roles of the burglars can be referring to the cues the teacher has written on the blackboard as a reminder.

The discussion should be spontaneous and fun for all participants. Students should be encouraged to embellish and add any original comments they feel like contributing.

Variations

i A panel discussion may be set up in which both burglars and police officers participate. The burglars will give bad advice, and the police officers will be responsible for refuting their advice.

Example: BURGLAR 1: People going on vacation shouldn't have their blinds up. They should leave them down so the house will have a closed-up look.

OFFICER 1: That's ridiculous! Everybody knows that the blinds should be left up slightly to give the house a less closed-up look.

ii Elements from the text can be used for dialogue practice done in pairs.

Using the cues on the blackboard, one pair partner tells why he had a bad vacation. The other pair partner gives him advice for the future.

Example: PAIR PARTNER 1: I didn't have a mechanical safety check done on my car and it broke down while we were on vacation.
PAIR PARTNER 2: You should always have a safety check done on your car before you leave on vacation. You should know that.
PAIR PARTNER 1: I didn't cancel deliveries to my house and the burglars knew I was away, so my house was robbed.
PAIR PARTNER 2: You ought to cancel all deliveries. Then burglars think you are home and stay away from your house.

The teacher should go around the class, monitoring the pair dialogues. Grammar errors should be corrected immediately.

Afterwards, one or two pair partners should be asked to perform their dialogues for the whole class.

Intensive Practice

I. Teacher explains that *do you think* and *should* are to be used in this exercise to form questions.

Individual students are called on to complete items 1–10.

II. Advice in the form of "don't you think you should" and the more direct "shouldn't you" are used in this exercise. Students are to respond to the statements using both forms.

The sample sentence is read by the teacher. The first sample answer is read by one student and the second sample answer by another student.

The teacher reads item 1 and a student gives appropriate advice using "Don't you think . . ."

Example: Don't you think you should see a doctor?

Then another student gives advice for the same item using "shouldn't you . . ."

Example: Shouldn't you see a doctor?

Items 2–10 are done similarly, with two students giving appropriate advice for the statement the teacher reads.

III. Students are to rephrase the sentences using "there ought to be. . ." in their sentences.

Teacher reads the example and then a student reads item 1 of the exercise.

Another student responds using "there ought to be . . ." (There ought to be a guard protecting the Embassy.)

Items 2–10 are done similarly.

IV. Students are told that they may either use "should" or "ought to" in their sentences. According to each student's personal opinion, he will begin with "I think . . ." or "I don't think . . ."

Teacher models the example and its two possible responses.

A student is called on to do item 1, saying something like "I don't think men should help their wives with the housework."

Teacher may ask the student why he holds that opinion, and then ask other students if they agree or disagree—and why.

Item 2 is done by another student, with the teacher soliciting different opinions from the rest of the class.

V. Exercise V provides an opportunity for students to express their ideas on controversial subjects while using "should" in the passive.

Since students usually have different opinions on most of the subjects, the exercise usually takes a long time. The teacher should take advantage of the opportunity to have students practice expressing their personal views.

The teacher may choose to put the two lists on the blackboard so that students will be looking up from the book.

The teacher should first introduce essential "language of expressing opinions"—phrases such as: "I believe," "In my opinion," "As far as I'm concerned." Also language of disagreement such as: "I disagree entirely," "I don't agree with you."

Students are told that according to their own personal beliefs, they are to match a controversy in list on the left with an item in list on the right, justifying their opinion.

Teacher elicits an opinion from one of the students, and then involves other class members.

Example: TEACHER: Carla, what do you think about examinations?
STUDENT: Well, I think examinations should be compulsory because students won't study unless they know they have to pass a test.
TEACHER: Miguel, what about you?
STUDENT: I disagree entirely. I believe exams should be abolished. They usually test what students don't know instead of what they do know.
TEACHER: Abdul, what about you?
STUDENT: Well, as far as I'm concerned, exams should be voluntary. If a student wants to improve his grade, he should be permitted to take an exam to raise his marks.

The other items are handled as described above. If a heated debate begins, the teacher should not interrupt for grammar correction, but take notes of any major grammar errors and discuss them afterwards.

Writing and Homework

I. Students are to fill in the blanks using either "should" or "ought to" and any other verbs and nouns necessary to complete the sentence.

Examples: 1. You should study harder. If not. . . .
2. Don't you think you ought to take your umbrella? It's. . . .

II. One or more items may be assigned to each student.

The student is to write a short paragraph of two or three lines, stating his opinion on the subject.

Students can follow the model paragraph shown at the beginning of the exercise. Item 2 might run as follows:

Problem children should be seen by a psychiatrist, since psychological problems only get worse with age. Professional help is needed to solve these children's problems, since most parents do not know how to deal with them.

III. The students are asked to read the situation silently in class and the teacher explains any vocabulary that students did not know.

Teacher may either assign both writing tasks to all students, or have students choose between them.

1. Students should be required to write a paragraph of at least three or four sentences, expressing their opinions on the situations given.

2. Students must write a dialogue between Gloria and Joanne in which they discuss the dilemma. An example would be:

JOANNE: Gloria, I think we have a problem.

GLORIA: What is it?

JOANNE: Well, you know that lottery ticket you wanted me to buy?

GLORIA: Sure. Did you buy it?

JOANNE: Yes, I bought two and . . . well, I've kept the tickets in my purse all this time and it seems that one of them has the winning number.

GLORIA: Oh, I understand. Now you don't know whose ticket has the winning number.

JOANNE: That's right. What do you think we should do?

Discussion

I. The students read the situation and the different opinions of Kenneth's relatives and acquaintances.

1. The teacher can either break the students up into groups of approximately four, or hold a discussion with the class as a whole giving its opinions.

   If students are working in groups, the group must come to a consensus about what Kenneth should do. Each group will report its decision to the whole class afterwards.

   If the class is working together, the students, after voicing their opinions, must come to a consensus on a plan of action for Kenneth.

2. The teacher divides the class into pairs. One pair member takes the role of Kenneth. The other pair partner is assigned the role of one of Kenneth's advisors (Reverend Brown, boss, brother, etc.)

   The family member or acquaintance will try to convince Kenneth to follow his or her advice. The pair partner playing Kenneth will have to raise objections to the person's advice.

   After the pairs have come to a decision, they will reenact their dialogues for the whole class.

   The teacher should be taking notes of major grammar errors to be discussed later.

II. This communication activity will follow a panel discussion format similar to the one in the **Expansion** section.

The students read the topic choices and pick one they find most appealing.

Before forming a circle for the panel discussion, each student should be allowed five or ten minutes to prepare notes on the topic.

A student is chosen to be the reporter/TV journalist who will conduct the discussion.

Students then form a circle and discuss the pros and cons of the topic they have chosen.

Teacher takes notes of major grammar errors as they occur, and discusses them afterwards.

Bits and Pieces

The teacher explains the two different uses of "supposed to" as given in the example.

The students read *John Howard's Wedding* silently and the teacher discusses unknown vocabulary afterwards with the whole class.

With students' books closed, the teacher may check comprehension by asking information questions such as:

TEACHER: Did Mrs. Dewhurst want her daughter to marry John?
STUDENT: No, she didn't.
TEACHER: How did John show up at the wedding?
STUDENT: In jeans and a sweater.
TEACHER: What time did he arrive?
STUDENT: At eleven.

The teacher may choose to have other students ask the questions.

Students are told to make comments on John's behavior, talking as if they were Mrs. Dewhurst. They should use "are supposed to" when referring to John's ignorance of correct behavior, and "were supposed to" when speaking of John's forgetfulness.

The students may consult the text to make the comments, or the teacher may put cues on the blackboard. The cues can include the type of mistake it was—"I" for incorrect procedure, and "F" for forgetfulness.

Examples:

blue jeans—I	marriage vows—I
11 o'clock—F	the aisle—I
guests' hands—F	limousine—F
"I do"—I	marriage certificate—F
kneel—I	

Using the cues, students form sentences speaking as Mrs. Dewhurst.

STUDENT 1—You're supposed to wear a tuxedo to a wedding, not blue jeans!
STUDENT 2—You were supposed to be there at 10 not 11, you idiot!

7   SPOT THE DANGERS

Presentation

The teacher explains that there are a lot of potential dangers in the two illustrations.

The teacher asks the students to look carefully at the Hospital Scene for a few minutes.

The teacher then asks the students to tell her what they found.

Examples: s1: There's a man refusing to take his medicine.
s2: One patient is smoking.
s3: It's very windy and cold because a window is open.
s4: There's a banana peel on the floor, and a nurse is about to step on it.

The teacher helps students discover dangers they may not have seen, and provides any vocabulary students might not know.

The teacher then asks the students to think of what will happen if the potential dangers actually occur. Students are told that they may express this cause/effect relationship using "if" followed by the present tense and the verb with "will" or "won't" in the main clause.

Using the example, the teacher illustrates the above point.

The teacher then calls on individual students to make up cause/effect statements based on the dangers in the first picture. Since each cause/effect can be expressed in a variety of ways, the teacher should elicit as many variations as possible.

Examples: s1: If the patient keeps on smoking, he won't get well.
s2: If the patient doesn't stop smoking, he'll get worse.
s3: If the patient smokes any more, he'll get worse.
(open window)
s1: If they don't close the window, the patients will get pneumonia.
s2: If the window stays open, several patients will catch cold.
s3: If somebody doesn't close the window soon, the patients will catch cold.

The teacher follows the same procedure as described above for the Home Scene.

Variations

After the students have done the exercise as described above, the teacher may ask the class to take the parts of nurses and patients who call out warnings to each other, based on the cues in the hospital scene.

Example: NURSE: Mr. Smith! If you don't take your medicine, you'll get worse!
PATIENT: Nurse, watch out! If you step on that banana peel you'll drop your tray and fall on that man with the broken leg!

Expansion

The teacher explains that the play is about five people who are planning to rob a bank. The characters are discussing potential problems. The teacher should also explain that in colloquial English the word "job" often means "robbery."

Students read the play silently. Teacher explains difficult vocabulary.

The teacher asks information questions to check students' comprehension.

Examples: Why were the robbers afraid of the bank camera?
Why couldn't they go through the side window?
Why did Angela want them to wear masks?

I. The same reading techniques as outlined for the play in chapter 4 (**Expansion**—The Hijacking) can be used, as well as the variations.

II. Students are called on to read the examples.

Individual students are chosen to do items 1–8. The teacher should fully exploit possible variations for each item.

Intensive Practice

I. The teacher explains the meaning of "what if" to the students, referring to the explanation given at the beginning of the exercise.

Student pairs are called on to do both examples. One student is to read the sentence on the left, and the other must formulate a response from the cues on the right.

Teacher then calls on student pairs to do items 1–10.

II. Students are told that both affirmative clauses must be put in the negative.

Students are called on to read the two examples.

Individual students are chosen to do items 1–10.

The teacher should insist that the students use the will + not = won't contraction.

III. Students are told that they are to formulate sentences with "as soon as" (B) based on the cue sentence (A). The students in B are given the framework for their responses, but they must provide an original verb and transform the subject pronoun into an object pronoun.

A student pair is called on to do example 1 and another student pair reads example 2.

Other student pairs are chosen to do items 1–10, with one student reading part A and the other formulating a response on the framework given.

Examples: 1. s1: Mark will get here soon.
      s2: As soon as he gets here, we'll tell him the good news.
   2. s1: Jane will arrive soon.
      s2: As soon as she arrives, we'll give her the birthday present.
   3. s1: Frank and Margaret will phone soon.
      s2: As soon as they phone, we'll give them the message.

IV. This exercise is a matching activity. Students are asked to read silently both sides of the chart which has "if-clauses" on the left, and future tense clauses on the right.

Students are then called on individually to read each item on the left and find any logical match on the right. There are several variations.

Example: 1. If my mother-in-law comes to visit, I'll go crazy.
or
If my mother-in-law comes to visit, I'll go out and celebrate.

After individual students have orally joined all the items in column one with those in column two, the teacher asks the students to think of comical combinations.

The teacher can provide an example such as:

If my mother-in-law comes to visit, she'll bite the mailman.

Individual students are called on to give their comical versions of each item.

V. The teacher discusses the idea of New Year's resolutions with the students, asking them if they have ever made such resolutions.

A short discussion can follow with students talking about resolutions they have made and either kept or broken.

The teacher then explains that a father and his son are making New Year's resolutions.

A son/father pair is chosen to read the example.

New son/father pairs are chosen to develop mini-dialogues using the cues provided. The pairs may choose cues randomly, or the teacher may want to have the students go down the list in order.

Example: FATHER: If you don't play your records so loud, I won't make you study on the weekend.
SON: OK, Dad. And I won't come home so late if you don't interrupt my phone calls.

Writing and Homework

I. The students must fill in the blanks with verbs and any other words necessary to complete the clause. Several variations are possible for each item.

Examples:

1. If it rains, we won't go to the beach.
   If it's not sunny, we won't go to the beach.
2. If he loses his job, he'll look for another one.
   If he loses his job, he'll be unhappy. . . .

II. Students are asked to write a chain dialogue in the first conditional, based on the information given in the dialogue shown. The example illustrates the technique.

There are several variations, but the dialogue may proceed as follows:

A: I'm going to take your ball away!
B: Oh yeah? If you take my ball away, I'll break your doll.
A: Try it! If you break my doll, I'll kick you!
B: Try it! If you kick me, I'll pull your hair!
A: If you pull my hair, I'll tear up your comic books!
B: If you tear up my comic books, I'll tell Mommy!

The students may want to perform the dialogues they have written for the whole class.

III. The students are told to write an informal letter to a friend following the instructions given.

Example:

Dear Françoise,

I was so glad to hear you are coming to visit! You asked me about transportation: well, I think that the train is the fastest way to get here. But remember, if you don't make your reservation early, there won't be any tickets. Also, don't forget to bring a bathing suit and a heavy sweater because although it's really hot during the day, you'll be cold if you don't wear a sweater at night. You asked how much money you should bring. I think $200 should be enough; but bring it in traveler's checks, because if they're stolen, you'll be able to get your money back.

Tell me when you're coming and I'll meet you at the station as soon as you arrive. When you're here we'll have a good time! As soon as you come, I'll take you to the Red Dragon Restaurant near my house. If the weather's nice, we'll go to Travis Beach. . . .

Discussion

I. Students are asked to read the comment. Discussion I is designed to have students express their opinions on zero population growth, a controversial issue in most countries.

The teacher can solicit individual students' opinions on the subject in a free discussion format, taking note of any grammar errors that arise for later discussion.

Or, the teacher may choose to divide the class into two debate teams—one for, one against the law. Each team should be given about 10–15 minutes to plan its debate strategy. Each team is then given a few minutes to present its argument, with individual team members expressing major points. After the major points have been aired, an open debate can begin. The teacher will act as arbiter and then decide which team's argument was the most convincing.

II. 1. Individual students are asked to read aloud the pro and con comment for item 1.

Students then discuss the advantages and disadvantages inherent in each one of the comments, and come to a decision as to which comment is the most valid.

Or, students can be broken into two hospital committee groups. One hospital committee is in favor of unlimited visiting privileges, and the other, against. Each group will be given from 10 to 15 minutes to plan a debate strategy. Each group will then present its arguments to the class.

2. These quotes may be handled as suggested for No. 1.

3. One student is asked to read each quote. The class then discusses both opinions on nurses and the nursing profession.

Bits and Pieces

I. Students are asked to read the text.
The teacher may wish to put cues on the blackboard.

Examples: plane trip, finding his way around, hotel, money, etc.

Students are told that they are to create dialogues between Mr. and Mrs. Harris, using the cues. Mrs. Harris' lines will begin with "what if" and Mr. Harris will respond in the first conditional.

A student pair is chosen to read the model dialogue.

Other pairs are selected to make original, 4-line dialogues based on the other cues.

II. Teacher reads the explanation of "No wonder" to the class.

Individual students are called on to do each of the two examples.

Individual students provide a logical sentence with "No wonder" for each of the items from 1 to 16.

Several variations are possible for each, and the teacher should solicit different variations.

Examples: 1. s1: No wonder he died immediately! She. . . .
s2: No wonder he was dead when he got to the hospital! She. . . .
2. s1: No wonder he got sick! He spent. . . .
s2: No wonder he caught a cold! He spent. . . .
s3: No wonder he got pneumonia! He spent. . . .

8   NUMEROLOGY

Presentation

I. Teacher gives a brief explanation of numerology by referring to the definition given in the text. Students are then shown how to find their personal numbers. An example can be done on the blackboard, or the teacher can refer to the examples shown in the text.

Each student then finds his personal number. Some students, especially those from Latin countries, may have exceptionally long names. If this is the case, the student(s) can be told to calculate their personal number using those name(s) they commonly go by or by using the name they feel most people know them by.

Students then read the meanings of numbers 1 to 9 silently and the teacher explains new vocabulary.

Students take turns asking each other about their personal numbers as shown in the example provided.

Variations

i. For more structured practice in the use of gerund constructions, the teacher can ask the students to close their books and elicit statements about each number using slash cues written on the blackboard. Students have to supply the gerunds.

Example:

Cues on Blackboard	Student responses
enjoy/leaders	Ones enjoy being leaders.
insist on/their own way	They insist on having their own way.
love/responsibilities	They love taking on responsibilities.
are criticized for/domineering	They are criticized for being domineering.
rarely admit/wrong	They rarely admit being wrong.
never stop/to reach their goals	They never stop trying to reach their goals.

The teacher can continue with cues made from the rest of the numbers

ii. Students can be asked to find the personal numbers of family members—father, mother, brother, etc. They then take turns asking each other about that person.

Example:

A: What's your mother's personal number?
B: She's a nine.
A: Is she an intellectual?
B: Well, in my opinion she's a very intelligent woman.
A: Does she insist on reading only the best books?

iii. Guessing Game (an idea for an exceptionally proficient class)

The students are asked to think of a very famous personality. (The teacher stipulates if the person is living or dead.)

Without telling their classmates who they chose, each student works out the personal number of the personality chosen.

Each student is then called on and, without saying the name of the famous person, tells in what way the number description coincides with the person's personality.

Example:

STUDENT 1: My famous person was a seven. He was accused of being a non-conformist and a dreamer, but he didn't like wearing strange clothes. In fact, he usually dressed conservatively, in black most of the time. He was criticized for being radical, especially by the politicians in the south of his country. He fought hard for his goals, but he understood the reason behind some of the conservative ideas of his countrymen. He was deep and philosophical, but down-to-earth and kind. He had trouble getting to know people because he was shy and reserved and conscious of his poor background.
STUDENT 2: Is your person Abraham Lincoln?
STUDENT 1: Yes.

As can be seen from the example, students should be encouraged to add information that will help the others guess the person's identity.

Expansion

Students read "The Hitchhiker" silently and the teacher explains difficult vocabulary.

Teacher checks for comprehension by asking such questions as: Where was John going? Why did he pick up the hitchhiker? What made him nervous about the hitchhiker?

I. Teacher explains the idea of the exercise and models the example. Individual students then do the exercise items.

II. This activity can be done spontaneously, the teacher calling on John/Martha pairs to come to the front of the class to talk about John's experience.

Or, student pairs can practice short dialogues for about fifteen minutes and then perform them for the rest of the class. Students can be asked to write the dialogues for homework.

Intensive Practice

I. Students are told that they have to supply a logical verb/gerund in each of the 10 exercise items. Teacher models the example and then calls on individual students to do the exercise.

II. Again students supply a logical verb/gerund after the expression "I'm thinking of." Cues can also be written on flashcards.

The teacher can use magazine pictures as flashcards to extend the exercise.

Example: (picture of a house)   STUDENT: I'm thinking of buying a house.
(picture of a concert)   STUDENT: I'm thinking of going to a concert.
(picture of a wedding)   STUDENT: I'm thinking of getting married.

The phrase "but I'm not sure yet" can be added to the responses.

III. Teacher explains that the sentences in the exercise have to be combined, the verb in parentheses being incorporated into the first clause as shown in the example. After modeling the example, teacher calls on individual students to do the exercise.

IV. Students do the exercise first with "accused of" and then with "arrested for." The verbs in parentheses are changed to gerunds in the exercise items.

V. After modeling the example, teacher calls on individual students to do the exercise items with "look forward to" and "enjoy."

As shown in the example, students are required to use a gerund construction in the first sentence and the present perfect with a gerund construction in the second sentence.

VI. The short quotations on the left provide the framework for statements which students must make using the cues on the right. After modeling the example, the teacher calls on individual students to do the exercise.

VII. Students have to invent an appropriate comment to follow the expression "what's the use of." The first part of the sentence supplied in the exercise establishes a context for students' comments.

A variety of answers is possible after each item. The example gives a clear idea of what the students are expected to do in the exercise.

For example, number 1 could be: Nobody will believe you, so what's the use of going to the police.
   telling them your story.
   insisting you're right.

Writing and Homework

   I. Students have to supply a logical gerund form to complete the exercise items and in most cases a few additional words.

Example: No. 1: She apologized for insulting the hostess
                                  breaking the vase
                                  coming so late

  II. Students read the story silently, ignoring the verbs in the parentheses and teacher explains difficult vocabulary.

Students are told that the story has to be rewritten to incorporate the verbs in parentheses. The original meaning of the story will stay the same, but many changes will have to be made in the text, as the example shows.

 III. Students have to write short paragraphs describing the personalities of people born under each of the zodiac signs listed.

Adjectives have been supplied to provide orientation for the students who are also told to use the verbs and expressions shown when possible.

The example illustrates a possible description of people born under the sign of Capricorn.

Variations

The students can also do a personal profile of a friend or family member who exemplifies the traits of a certain sign. They are told to use the adjective and the verbs and expressions provided in their personality profile.

Example: My friend Ann is an Aries. She's the most active and lively person I know. She loves traveling and hates sitting around the house. Being domineering, she insists on doing everything her way. . .

Discussion

These three discussion areas may be done on the same day of class or each one can be used as a 15 minute "finish-up" to three separate lessons.

   I. 1. Teachers can use the adjective descriptions for the signs of the zodiac in exercise III of the **Writing and Homework** section as a basis for discussion or another source with more complete descriptions.

Each student talks about the description given for his (or her) sign and tells whether he (or she) thinks it is accurate or not.

      2. Teacher calls for individual opinions and encourages an exchange of ideas among students. Teacher and/or students can bring to class such supplementary materials as books, articles, or tarot cards to talk about.

      3. The student is asked about occult practices or beliefs particular to his or her country. The teacher may wish to have students prepare this topic before class discussion takes place.

  II. These two topics should both be discussed in the same class.

      1. Students are asked to give individual opinions or the class can be divided into two groups, one discussing the advantages of hitchhiking and the other, the disadvantages. After talking in their groups for 10 or 15 minutes, students then debate the issue in class.

      2. Students tell about their own experiences or about things that have happened to people they know.

Bits and Pieces

Teacher reads the situation with the students and goes over the 13 items.
  I. Students first make polite requests using "would you mind" and then, more impolite orders as shown in the example.
 II. The same procedure is followed as in I, this time with the students formulating requests and orders in the negative. Again, 2 examples have been provided.

9   THINK FAST

Presentation

The teacher explains that the instructors in the pictures are giving lessons and asking questions about emergency or unexpected situations.

The teacher asks the students to look over the cues in each drawing. New vocabulary is explained.

The teacher points out that in hypothetical situations such as these, the verb in the "if" clause is in the past tense, while the conditional "would + verb" is used in the other clause.

The teacher gives the students one or two examples of how to formulate the questions. (What would you do if a hijacker tried to take your plane to a different destination? What would you do if a passenger became sick?)

The teacher then has the students continue asking, "What would you do if" questions, based on the rest of the cues in the two illustrations.

When all the questions have been practiced, the teacher calls on a student pair to model the example for picture A.

Two other students are then chosen to take the parts of the flight attendant instructor and one of his pupils. The instructor's question is based on one of the blackboard cues, and the student uses his imagination to formulate the answer.

New student pairs are chosen. Different pairs do the question asking and answering until all the cues in both drawings have been used.

Variations

Students can be divided into groups of three, taking the parts of an instructor and two students with conflicting ideas.

The teacher assigns several different cues to each group (group 1—1st three cues in picture A; group 2, next three cues in picture A . . . etc.)

After answering the instructor's question, each student defends his answer and tries to discredit that of his colleague. The instructor acts as an arbiter.

Example: INSTRUCTOR: What would you do if a hijacker tried to force the pilot to fly to a different destination?
s1: Well, I'd follow his instructions exactly. These people are dangerous.
s2: *I'd* try and talk to him and persuade him to give up the idea.
s1: That's a dangerous thing to do. What if he decided to use violence? . . .

After practicing the exchanges in their groups, students can then perform the conversations for the rest of the class.

Expansion

The students read the play silently, and teacher deals with vocabulary difficulties.

To check student understanding of the play, teacher asks such information questions as:

Where does the story take place?

Why was Peggy nervous about meeting Jack?

What suggestions did her friends give her?

I. The same memorization technique as outlined for the play in chapter 4 (**Expansion** section) can be used, as well as the variations. You may want to tape the play as well.

II. This can be done as a spontaneous role-play with several students performing the parts of Jack and his friends for the rest of the class.

The whole class can then discuss the effectiveness of the solutions given.

Teacher should note down errors as they occur and deal with them later.

Teacher can have groups of students write a short conversation for this situation which they can rehearse and then perform for each other.

Intensive Practice

I. Teacher explains that "If I were you. . . ." is often used when giving advice, and models the example.

Students are then called on to do the exercise.

Cues can be written on flashcards if the teacher wishes.

II. Students have to ask questions based on the short situations given in the exercise.

The example shows how the question is to be formulated.

III. Using the skeleton setences provided, the student formulates a conditional sentence for each of the people listed on the left.

The clauses will either be affirmative or negative, depending on the cues in the skeleton sentence.

Teacher first models the two examples given.

IV. Students have to rephrase the exercise items, using "if."

The two examples shown give a clear idea of what is expected in the exercise.

V. Students must ask a "What would you do if . . ." question which would logically lead to the responses in the exercise.

There are several possible questions for each item.

Writing and Homework

I. Students have to fill in the blanks with words or phrases that will correctly complete each item.

II. Students have to choose what they consider to be the right answer to each question, and then explain what would happen if one or the other procedures were followed.

Answers: 1-C /2-B / 3-D / 4-A

An example might be:

If a friend of mine got an electrical shock, I would turn the electricity off at the source. If I tried to pull him away, I would get electrocuted too.

III. The students are to compose short advice letters for the ten problems listed in the exercise. Students may either choose one or two letters they would like to write, or the teacher may assign one or two of the problems to each student.

When the assignments have been corrected, the teacher can read especially imaginative or well thought-out letters to the rest of the class.

The correction technique mentioned in the **Writing and Homework** section of Chapter 3 (exercise III) can be used.

Discussion

I. The teacher reads each of the quotations with the students and encourages discussion by asking what they would do in these situations.

After the students have discussed what they would do, the teacher may choose to have the students do quick role-plays based on situations 1, 3, 4, and 5.

1. The teacher has several students enact the elevator scene. Though there will be little talking and much pandemonium, the exercise is good for student morale.

3. The teacher chooses a student to play Rafael Fuentes, the stranger, and any other character Fuentes might tell his problem to.

4. The teacher chooses a student to play Bob Croft, the sleeping student, and then, perhaps, a Bob Croft/colleague pair who will discuss Bob's problem and/or teaching methodology!!

5. The teacher chooses a priest/parishioner pair. The priest will try to convince the parishioner-murderer to reconsider his decision.

II. 1. When the students have done the First Aid quiz (**Writing and Homework,** exercise II) for homework, or in class as a writing exercise, the teacher can discuss student answers with the class, and ask what would happen if one of the wrong procedures were followed.

2. The students can be asked to read *The Reunion* again for ideas.

Five or six class members are then asked to come to the front of the room, and spontaneously enact the new situation.

Or, students may be put into groups of four or five, in which one of the group members will be the rich person.

The group should hold a spontaneous discussion with the rich person telling his (or her) problem and friends giving advice.

During the discussion, the students can be taking simple notes on what was said.

Based on the notes and what they remember of the discussion, each group can be asked to report its discussion for the whole class.

Variations

The class as a whole, or groups of four or five, can be asked to rewrite the play *The Reunion,* reversing the theme. Students will refer to the play and discuss appropriate revisions.

The teacher will collect each group's rewritten play, correct it, and ditto or photocopy it for the whole class, if possible.

The students as a whole can pick the best of the plays and if they wish, perform it in class.

Bits and Pieces

I. The teacher explains that *had better/had better not* is used to express strong advice or warning, and reminds students that Mrs. Harris was the woman in Chapter 7 who was worried about her son's trip to Europe.

After modeling the example, the teacher calls on individual students to do each item.

Several variations are possible for each item. The teacher should solicit as many variations as possible.

Example: The flights usually fill up fast in August so you'd better make your reservation now.

or

The flights usually fill up fast in August so you'd better not wait too long to make a reservation.

10   PEOPLE AND PASTIMES

Presentation

Teacher explains that the people in the illustrations were interviewed on a "talk show" called *Faces in Focus* where they were asked about their professions and hobbies.

Teacher then elicits each character's profession and hobby (or special interest) as the students refer to the illustrations and the cues beside each picture. Students can also ask each other about the characters.

Example: TEACHER (OR STUDENT): What does Sam Segovia do for a living?
STUDENT: He's president of Apex Incorporated.
TEACHER (OR STUDENT): And what about his hobby?
STUDENT: He plays the guitar.

Teacher explains that the cues show the length of time each character has been practicing his hobby or working at his profession—and emphasizes that each one is *still* doing these things.

Teacher points out that the present perfect continuous tense is used here for actions begun in the past but which continue into the present.

Teacher elicits "how long" questions as students ask about the hobbies and professions of the characters. At this point, only the questions are practiced.

Example: STUDENT 1: How long has Sam Segovia been president of Apex Inc.?
STUDENT 2: How long has he been playing the guitar?

Teacher explains the difference between "for" and "since," pointing out that "for" is used to show duration of time (for 3 years, for 2 weeks, for 6 months) and "since" shows the starting point of the action (since 1975, since he was a child, since last October).

Students then tell how long each character has been practicing his hobby or profession, referring to the cues beside the pictures. Students make "for" sentences from the first cue and "since" sentences from the other.

Example: STUDENT 1: Sam Segovia has been president of Apex Inc. for 5 years.
STUDENT 2: He has been playing the guitar since he was 16 years old.

I. Students read the sample dialogue silently for comprehension.

Teacher chooses two students to model the sample dialogue.

Teacher chooses another student pair to read the dialogue, this time taking the roles of David Snow and one of the other characters.

This procedure is repeated until all the characters have been used.

II. Students ask and answer questions about the characters as shown in the example.

III. When all the previously outlined work has been done and students are able to manipulate the structure with ease, they are divided into pairs.

One pair partner takes the role of David Snow, and the other, of one of the characters in the illustration.

If there are more than ten students in the class, the same character roles can be assigned to more than one pair until the whole class is involved.

Interviewers are encouraged to ask anything they want and the characters have to invent appropriate answers.

This exercise works best when done spontaneously, with the teacher noting down grammar errors to be discussed later.

Expansion

Students read the play *Myrtle Meets a Movie Star* silently and teacher explains new vocabulary.

Teacher asks comprehension questions about the play, such as: Why did Myrtle want to go to the restaurant? What did she try to find out from the waiter? Why did they stay in the restaurant so long?

Students read the play aloud, taking the parts of the characters.

A restaurant scene is set up as indicated in the instructions to the activity following the play.

Students take the parts of the characters and re-enact the play referring only to the cues shown. Since students will not always be able to remember dialogue from the play, they can use their own words as long as they follow the outline.

Teacher should note down present perfect errors and any other major errors to be discussed later.

This exercise can be done twice if the class is big, to include all students.

Variations

Students can perform the play by following the technique outlined in Chapter 4 (**Expansion** section).

If recording equipment is available, a tape can be made of the performance, which the students and teacher can later discuss.

Intensive Practice

I. Students have to answer the 10 questions which form the exercise using the cues on the right. They will have to use "for" or "since" depending on the cue, or "all" + a time period.

Three sample questions and answers are shown in the example. The teacher reads the questions, and asks students to model the sample answers.

Students then answer the 10 exercise questions using the cues on the right. Or, for variety, the cues can be put on flashcards or written on the blackboard. With students' books closed, the teacher reads each question and shows or points to an appropriate cue.

II. Students have to complete the exercise items supplying a logical verb in the present perfect and either "for" or "since."

Teacher models the 2 sentences in the example and students then do the exercise items.

The exercise items can also be put on flashcards.

III. This time the students formulate questions with "how long" and an appropriate verb in the present perfect.

Teacher models the example and individual students are called on to complete the exercise.

IV. "Know," "have," and "be," which are not used in the continuous form, are practiced in this exercise.

Students complete the three groups of exercises using the present perfect and the verb indicated.

The example gives a clear idea of what is expected in the exercise.

V. Students have to ask questions using "how long" + the present perfect and give answers according to the cues provided.

The teacher explains that "ever since," which is to be used in the answers, is more emphatic than "since."

A student models the question in the example, and another student reads the answer.

Student pairs then ask and answer the 10 questions in the exercise.

Question cues can be written on flashcards with corresponding answer cues written on the back.

VI. Students have to invent an appropriate question after reading the responses supplied. They use the present perfect in their questions and the word "long" at the end, as shown.

After going over the example, teacher calls on individual students to do the exercise.

Writing and Homework

I. Students fill in the blanks with the present perfect and an appropriate verb.

II. Students write about the inventions listed in the exercise as shown in the example.

Some of their sentences should be modeled after the first example, and others after the second example.

III. Students have to write 10 facts about themselves using the present perfect for activities/actions that are still continuing. A sample beginning has been provided.

Discussion

I. The class is divided into pairs with one partner taking the role of the reporter and the other, one of the people to be interviewed.

The reporter should introduce himself and his subject to the rest of the class and then ask questions first about the person's professional life, and then about his or her hobby.

Other class members can also ask questions if they wish.

II. The teacher chooses a student to take the part of Elizabeth Gaynor and explains to the class that they are about to interview a famous movie star about her life and career.

The student playing the part of Elizabeth Gaynor may keep her book open and refer to the information. Other students, however, must close their books.

Students ask the movie star anything they like about her life, interests and hobbies, films, present activities, marriage(s), children, etc.

Elizabeth Gaynor should feel free to add any original information she wishes.

Afterwards students can write a newspaper article based on the interview.

Michael Newbury—the same procedure is followed as outlined above.

Bits and Pieces

Teacher goes over the use of "ever since" by referring to the explanation given. After modeling the examples, teacher explains that students are to make sentences with "ever since" and the present perfect based on the movie stars' quotes in the exercise.

Individual students model the two examples and then do the exercise.

11   DARLING ROSEMARY AND DEAREST BILL

Presentation

Referring to the short situation outlined in the text, the teacher explains that Bill and Rosemary, an engaged couple, have not been true to each other.

Teacher also points out that they have not been telling the truth in their letters.

Students read both letters silently and the teacher explains any difficult vocabulary.

Teacher points out that the present perfect is used with "recently" and "lately" for actions that began in the past but which are still continuing, even though the words "recently" and "lately" are sometimes omitted.

Teacher may want to write cues on the blackboard from the two letters and elicit recently/lately statements from the students.

Example: (Bill's letter to Rosemary)

Board cues	*Student responses*
I/busy lately	I've been busy lately.
I/every night until 2:00 a.m.	I've been studying every night until 2:00 a.m.
Professor Smiley/us a lot of work to do	Professor Smiley has been giving us a lot of work to do.
I/most of my free time in the library and biology lab	I've been spending most of my free time in the library and biology lab.
I/cheese sandwiches and I/	I've been eating cheese sandwiches

black coffee to stay awake

and drinking black coffee to stay awake.

I/a lot of headaches lately.

I've been getting a lot of head-aches lately.

What/you/doing?

What have you been doing?

(the same procedure can be followed for Rosemary's letter to Bill)
For further practice, the teacher can elicit statements about Bill's and Rosemary's actions using short oral cues.

Examples:

Cue	Student response
2:00 a.m.	He's been studying until 2:00 every night.
Professor Smiley	Professor Smiley has been giving him a lot of work to do.
library	He's been spending most of his free time in the library.

I. Students reread the letters and then look at the photo albums which show what Bill and Rosemary have really been doing.

Teacher elicits recently/lately statements about each picture. The words "recently" and "lately" can be omitted

Examples:

(Bill's album)
(picture 1) STUDENT 1: He's been going to parties.
(picture 2) STUDENT 2: He's been going out with /going to the movies with a girl named Cheryl.
(picture 3) STUDENT 3: He's been skiing with a girl named Diana.
(picture 4) STUDENT 4: He's been playing poker.

(the same procedure can be followed for Rosemary's album)

II. Students are told that Bill and Rosemary have just discovered the truth about each other.

Students conduct a phone conversation in which each person angrily accuses the other of being untrue.

Two students first model the example which uses information from the first pictures in each album.

The teacher then calls on another two students to do a similar short dialogue, this time based on the *second* pictures in each album.

This procedure is repeated until all pictures have been used.

Variations

i. After following the procedure outlined for I, the teacher can elicit longer statements from students, referring to both the letter and the album.

Examples:

Cue (on blackboard or flashcards)	Student response
study/parties	He hasn't been studying every night! He's been going to parties.
work/Cheryl	He hasn't been working hard! He's been going out with a girl named Cheryl.
library/Diane	He hasn't been spending his free time in the library! He's been skiing with Diane.
sandwiches and black coffee/poker	He hasn't been living on sandwiches and black coffee! He's been playing poker.

(similar cues can be made from Rosemary's letter)

ii. Bill/Rosemary student pairs may plan a phone conversation using all the information in the letters and the albums.

After practicing for 10 to 15 minutes, pairs perform their dialogues for the rest of the class. Students can be encouraged to add original comments if they wish.

The dialogues can be assigned for homework or for in-class writing.

iii. If there is an unequal balance of men and women in the class, pairs composed of two men or two women can practice the following dialogue instead of the one outlined above.

One student takes the part of a friend of Bill's and the other, a friend of Rosemary's. Each person tries to blame the other's friend for the situation.

Sample dialogue:

BILL'S FRIEND: That Rosemary! She hasn't been working late every night. She's been having dinner with her boss at expensive restaurants.

ROSEMARY'S FRIEND: All right, but what about Bill? He hasn't been studying for his final exams. He's been going to parties.

The two friends continue the dialogue referring to the information in the letters and the photo album.

iv. As a follow-up writing activity, students can be asked to compose a letter to an advice column written by either Bill or Rosemary explaining that his (or her) fiancé has been untrue and asking for advice.

After correcting the letters, the teacher can read especially good ones to the whole class.

Expansion

I. Students first read the play *Middleton's Mysterious Virus* silently for comprehension. Teacher then explains problem vocabulary.

Teacher asks (or students ask each other) questions about the play such as:

Why were they waiting to see the doctor?

What symptoms did they have?

Why did everyone think it was a virus?

Students then take the parts of the different characters and read the play aloud.

The parts can be reassigned to include any students who were left out, and read again.

Teacher can isolate certain lines, model the intonation, and have students try to imitate.

II. Teacher assigns the roles of Mr. Jacobson, Mr. DiAngelo, Mr. Carver, Mrs. Simpson, Mrs. White, and Chef LePierre to six students who come to the front of the room and argue about the problem outlined in the text.

Teacher can also describe each character to guide the students' dialogue.

Example: MR. JACOBSON: angry, accusing, emotional
MR. DIANGELO: hesitant, unwilling to blame Chef LePierre
MR. CARVER: uncomfortable, doesn't like "scenes," conciliatory
MRS. SIMPSON: angry, insistent
MRS. WHITE: calm, logical, rational
CHEF LEPIERRE: defensive, argumentative

After students have performed the conversation, the teacher can correct errors from notes that she has made.

Variations

i. If the teacher wishes to provide more practice in the structure, statements, and questions with the present perfect continuous and/or "recently" and "lately" can be elicited from the play dialogue with blackboard or flashcard cues.

Example:

Cue	Student response
A mysterious virus/around Middleton lately	A mysterious virus has been going around Middleton lately.
I/awful lately	I've been feeling awful lately.
I/stomach cramps/3 weeks/last month	I've been getting/suffering from stomach cramps for 3 weeks/since last month.
I/2 hours of sleep	I've been getting 2 hours of sleep.
What/you/yourself/lately	What have you been doing with yourself lately?
I/crazy	I've been going crazy.

ii. In a large class, students can be divided into groups of six and plan an argument between the 5 characters in the doctor's waiting room and Chef LePierre, as outlined in activity II.

After planning the conversation for about 15 minutes, students then perform the argument for the rest of the class.

Conversations can be assigned for homework or in-class writing.

Intensive Practice

I. Students have to make statements with "recently" or "lately" and the present perfect continuous. Verb cues are listed to the right of each exercise item.

Teacher models the example and individual students then do the exercise.

For variety, the verb cues on the right can be written on the blackboard, and the sentence cues on flashcards.

Teacher elicits statements by showing a flashcard and pointing to the appropriate verb.

As students get more proficient, teacher can erase the verb cues and elicit statements from the flashcards alone.

II. This exercise practices negative recently/lately statements.

The same procedure as outlined for I can be followed.

III. This substitution drill practices the question "What have you/has he, etc., been doing lately?" and a very common follow-up statement which appeared in the play in the **Expansion** section—"I haven't seen you/him, etc., in ages."

Teacher should practice the model with students several times and explain how the substitution works by referring to the example.

With students looking away from their books, the teacher gives the substitution cues in the exercise orally.

Students base their responses on the model, making necessary verb and pronoun changes.

The pace of this drill should be quick and the exercise can be done several times until students are proficient at making the transformations.

IV. Students have to ask questions and give answers using the present perfect continuous. The verbs to be used in the answers are cued on the right.

One student models the question in the example, and another student models the answer.

Pairs of students then ask and answer the questions in the exercise.

V. Students have to complete sentence 1 in the exercise so that it logically corresponds to sentence 2.

There are several variations for each item and the teacher should try to elicit as many as possible.

The example shows a possible response for "That's why you are gaining weight."

Writing and Homework

I. Students fill in the blanks of this doctor/patient dialogue using the present perfect continuous and the verb supplied.

Teacher may wish to have students practice this exercise orally.

II. Teacher explains the situation referring to the brief explanation provided.

Students then write conclusions as to what someone has been doing in their apartment, using the cues in the exercise.

III. Students have to write a letter as explained.

Teacher should instruct them to use the present perfect continuous when telling what they've been doing recently/lately, but explain that other verb tenses can also be used in the letter.

Discussion

I. Students work in pairs as explained in the exercise, the "doctor" asking questions about the "patient's" symptoms until he has enough information to diagnose the disease.

An example has been provided, showing a possible dialogue.

Students can continue the dialogue with the doctor prescribing treatment and the patient asking questions about his disease.

Teacher should go around listening to student pairs and make corrections of errors, especially those involving the present perfect.

Students then perform their dialogues for the rest of the class.

II. Teacher can elicit opinions from the whole class, asking students to give reasons for their beliefs.

When opinions differ, teacher should encourage everyone to take sides and get involved in the discussion.

Teacher should take notes of major grammar errors and discuss them with the class later.

Bits and Pieces

I. Teacher explains the meaning of "How about . . . ing" by referring to the short explanation and example in the text.

Teacher then explains that students have to take the parts of Mr. and Mrs. Benson who are going to celebrate their fiftieth wedding anniversary.

Mrs. Benson makes suggestions using "How about . . . ing." Mr. Benson agrees, saying, "That's a good idea!" and continues with "It's been a long time since I __"

The example shows how the exchange should go.

One student models Mrs. Benson's suggestion in the example, and another student models Mr. Benson's response.

Student pairs then take the parts of Mr. and Mrs. Benson and do the exercise.

The teacher may wish to go through the exercise first with "How about . . . . ing," then with "It's been a long time since I . . .," and finally combine the question and response.

II. Teacher explains the expression "in (for) ages" by referring to the short explanation and example in the text.

Students do exercise I again, this time using "I haven't . . . . in (for) ages" for Mr. Benson's responses.

Teacher may wish to practice this phrase before having students do the Benson dialogue. Short cues can be written on the blackboard or given orally to prompt "I haven't . . . in (for) ages" sentences.

Example:

Cue	Student response
Chinese food	I haven't eaten/had Chinese food in (for) ages.
a good book	I haven't read a good book in (for) ages.
to a party	I haven't been to a party in (for) ages.
a good movie	I haven't been to/seen a good movie in (for) ages.

12 THE THEFT OF THE CENTURY

Presentation

I. Teacher explains the robbery plan by referring to the short situation at the beginning of the chapter.

Students are told that Mike Dobson is asking questions about Ted's experience.

Teacher models the example shown and students continue asking "Have you ever" questions using the cues beside the illustration.

When students are proficient at asking "Have you ever" questions, they are told that since Ted is a very inexperienced thief, he answers all of Mike's questions as shown in the example.

Teacher calls on one student to ask a "Have you ever" question and another to respond as Ted does. (Items 6, 10, and 11 are answered with just "No, I haven't.")

This procedure is repeated until all cues have been used.

II. Referring to the short situation outlined in the text, teacher explains that Ted is inside the Louvre about to steal the Mona Lisa, and that Mike is outside with a walkie-talkie asking him questions.

Teacher refers students to the checklist in the text and explains that each step in the operation has been precisely timed.

Teacher models Mike Dobson's first question shown in the example and calls on a student to give the affirmative answer "Yes, I have."

Teacher then calls on individual students to ask "Have you/yet?" questions using the cues on the checklist. Other students are called on to give the affirmative answer, "Yes, I have."

Teacher models the first negative response (b) and calls on students to make similar statements using the checklist.

The same procedure is followed for the other negative response (c).

Teacher then writes the following three cues on the blackboard: *Yes/No. . .yet/* and *No. . .still. . .*

One student is called on to ask a "Have you/yet?" question from the first cue on the checklist. Another student answers the question as the teacher points to one of the response cues on the blackboard.

This procedure is followed until all cues on the checklist have been used.

III. Teacher explains that Inspector Klutz of Interpol is watching and reporting on every move Ted makes inside the Louvre.

Teacher models the example referring students to the first and second items on the checklist.

Students then continue the report, referring to the rest of the checklist, two items at a time.

Expansion

I. Teacher explains any vocabulary from the text that the students might find difficult (humiliated, jerk, to lose one's temper, enroll, etc.).

Students read the story silently.

Teacher may then assign individual students character roles from the story. Students then read the text aloud.

Teacher or students can then ask comprehension questions about the story.

Examples: What happened when Clyde and Dorothy were at the beach one day?
What did Clyde read in the newspaper one evening?
How did Clyde treat Dorothy and his boss after he finished the course?

I. *Never*—Students make complete statements from the cues provided, using the verbs in parentheses.

The same procedure is followed for the other groups of sentences with "ever," "already," and "yet."

II. Students are divided into pairs, the teacher assigning one of the sets of characters shown to each pair.

Student pairs plan a short dialogue using information from the text and ideas of their own.

The dialogue should first be practiced spontaneously and then the students may write their lines.

After the teacher has corrected students' written work (this can be done in class as teacher goes around to each group), students are given a few minutes to practice the corrected version of their dialogues.

Students then perform their conversations for the whole class without referring to their notes.

Intensive Practice

I. Students ask questions with the present perfect and "yet" as shown in the example.

The verb to be used is in parentheses on the right.

Teacher models the example and students then do the exercise.

II. Students ask questions with the present perfect and "ever," supplying a logical verb.

A student is called on to read the example.

Students then do the 10 exercise items.

III. Students have to ask a question with "When . . . going to" and then give a response with the present perfect and "already."

Teacher models the question in the example and chooses a student to read the response.

Student pairs then ask and answer the questions cued in the exercise.

The exercise cues can also be put on flashcards so students will not have to constantly refer to the text.

IV. The statements in this exercise have to be completed in the negative with the present perfect and "yet."

Students use the cues in parentheses on the right to complete the statements.

Teacher models the example and calls on individual students to do the exercise items.

This drill can be done again, this time with the cues in parentheses covered up, to make the exercise more challenging.

V. This exercise practices the present perfect and "never."

Students have to supply the verb and use a question tag to end each sentence.

Teacher models the example and then calls on students to do the exercise.

VI. Teacher reads the short introductory situation and explains that the exercise shows the mayor's campaign slogans when he was running for office. There is also a time element in parentheses below each slogan.

Students are told that Mayor Biggs has not kept his promises and that they have to complain about his lack of action using "still" and the present perfect.

One student is chosen to model the example.

Students then do the exercise items.

Teacher may wish to practice the two parts of each sentence separately before finally combining them.

Writing and Homework

I. Students complete the exercise with the present perfect, a logical verb, and any other necessary words.

II. 1. Students first complete the story using the present perfect and the verb provided. When each of the eight sections has been completed, students must rearrange them in correct order, and then write out the narrative.

2. Teacher reads the short situation outlined in the text and the dialogue example. Students are told to write the rest of the conversation asking questions with "yet" and the cues provided. Teacher should encourage students to try and make the dialogue sound natural, as shown in the example, by using their own ideas for comments and exclamations that Bob and Joanne might make as they talk to each other.

III. Students read Mayor Buster Biggs's speech silently and teacher explains new vocabulary.

By referring to the example in the text, teacher explains that a Buster Biggs supporter and a supporter of the opposing party are having an argument. The former is praising Mayor Biggs's accomplishments using "already" while the latter is criticizing his lack of action using the negative and "still."

Students have to write the rest of the conversation using the facts in Mayor Biggs's speech and their own ideas for extra comments.

After correcting the written conversations, teacher may wish to divide the class in half for some oral practice. One group is told that they have to defend Mayor Biggs, and the other that they have to attack him.

To guide the argument, students can refer to the following cues that the teacher writes on the blackboard:

+

new library	no new hospital
new city hall	no new recreation center
10 million dollars in outside	no gangsters in jail
investments for local	no rent control law
industry	no raise in city employees' salaries
clean streets	no credit extended to local farm-
no pollution	ers
a lower rate of unemployment	
inflation controlled	

Students then spontaneously carry on a discussion about Mayor Biggs, with the teacher deciding the "inner" on the basis of the effectiveness and forcefulness of the arguments.

Discussion

I. Teacher explains what a "confidence man" is by referring to the text.

Teacher emphasizes that these people are "smooth talkers" who are able to make even the most far-fetched schemes sound convincing.

Students are divided into pairs with one partner taking the role of a con man who has to persuade his partner to spend money on one of the schemes shown in the text.

The class as a whole can decide if they wish to prepare the dialogues first, or perform them spontaneously.

Teacher takes notes of major grammar errors to be discussed later.

Variations

Individual students or student pairs pretend they are con men.

After choosing one of the schemes shown in the text, students take 10 to 15 minutes to prepare a convincing sales pitch.

Students then come to the front of the room and give their "pitch" to the rest of the class. The class can ask questions after the initial presentation which the con man(men) will have to answer.

The class later decides which sales pitch was the most convincing.

II. Students read the situation outlined in the text. Teacher assigns student pairs one of the cities shown in the text and explains that one partner has to take the part of the mayor of that city, and the other, of his opponent in the coming elections.

Students are told that the two candidates are going to have a public pre-election debate.

The mayor will try and emphasize his main achievement while his opponent will concentrate on a serious problem that has not been resolved in the city.

Partners should separate and plan a strategy—i.e. a plan of attack and a plan of defense for the debate.

Pairs then come to the front of the room and carry on a debate, with the teacher (or another student) acting as moderator. There should be a preset time limit for the debates.

When each pair has finished, the teacher distributes "ballots" and the rest of the students "vote" for their favorite candidate.

Example: (*Discussion* section—II)

MAYOR OF MIDVILLE: Before I became mayor of this city, the streets were covered with garbage and I was very concerned for the health of all Midville citizens. We can't have children growing up in a dirty city. So the first thing I did was to improve garbage collection. I think everyone will agree that we now have the cleanest streets in the state!

OPPONENT: I agree with clean streets! Everyone agrees with clean streets—but Midville's biggest problem is its high crime rate. A crime takes place every hour in this city. Yes, we have clean streets, but who can walk on them after 10:00 at night? What have you done to fight crime in Midville?

MAYOR OF MIDVILLE: I have only been mayor for three years. All over this country crime is a major social problem which cannot be solved by one person in such a short time.

Bits and Pieces

I. Students are told that the expression "What does he(or she) look like?" refers to physical characteristics.

Teacher explains that the "Wanted" posters show members of the Dobson gang and that people are phoning the police to report that they have seen these criminals.

To make sure that the callers have the right person, Inspector Klutz asks for a general physical description (What does he(or she) look like:), and then for more detailed information as shown in the example.

Two students model the example and then two more students are called on to complete the sample conversation.

Pairs of students can then be assigned caller/Inspector Klutz roles as they talk about Ted Harris and Angela Nye.

Teacher monitors the pairs as they practice their dialogues, making corrections of errors.

Several pairs then "perform" the conversations for the whole class.

II. Teacher explains that "What is he(or she) like?" is used to ask for information about someone's personality.

Students are told to refer back to the zodiac descriptions in the **Writing and Homework** section of Chapter 8.

After choosing one of their relatives or friends whose sign they know, students ask about his(or her) personality using "What's he(or she) like?"

An example has been provided in the text of a possible dialogue.

13 WENDY STORM'S BAD YEAR

Presentation

I. The students are asked to read the introductory paragraph either aloud or silently.

New vocabulary is discussed.

Teacher asks information questions to check students' understanding of text.

Example: What is Wendy's profession?
Why has Wendy changed?
How has she been behaving lately?

Teacher points out that "last year" refers to a finished time in the past and requires the past tense. "This year," however, being unfinished time, calls for the present perfect tense.

Teacher calls students' attention to the fact that the chart is broken into last year (past tense) and this year (present perfect) categories, as well as "how many," "how many times," and "how much" categories.

Students are told that Wendy is talking to her agent who is trying to make her see how different this year has been from last year.

Students read the first cue, then two students are called on to read the sample dialogue.

Students are told that they must continue the dialogues, and that although the past tense/present perfect contrast must be used, they can add any other original information they like. The sample dialogue shows how additional information can be included. Phrases such as, "Wendy, don't you see . . . ," "the one with International Studios," "but it's because I didn't like the directors" are optional, but they make the dialogue sound more natural.

The teacher calls on two more students to do a dialogue based on cue two.

A dialogue with students providing extra comments and information may sound like this:

AGENT: Wendy, things keep on getting worse! Look, how many movies did you make last year?

WENDY: Well, I made four movies . . . and three TV specials.

AGENT: That's right . . . and how many movies have you made this year?

WENDY: Well, I've only made one movie so far this year, but that's your fault . . . you should try to find me better roles!
(the teacher may want to let the students go on)

AGENT: Better roles?! I've been trying to get work for you for months, but the directors won't hire you . . . you're unreliable!

Other student pairs are called on to perform the dialogues for the rest of the cues.

II. Students are told that now Wendy is talking to her director who is furious with her behavior.

Teacher asks students to look over the cues and reminds them that the past tense/present perfect contrast will have to be made. Students are reminded that they will have to use "how much," "how many," and "how many times," according to the cues. They should be encouraged to use their imaginations and add any extra comments or information they like.

Teacher may choose to write the cues for II on the blackboard.

Two students are selected to do a dialogue based on the first cue. The dialogue could read like this:

DIRECTOR: Wendy, I'm running out of patience! You keep on getting worse!
WENDY: What do you mean, Mr. Goldbin?
DIRECTOR: How many coffee breaks did you have last week?
WENDY: About 10.
DIRECTOR: Ten? You mean 30! And how many coffee breaks have you had this week?
WENDY: About 40!
DIRECTOR: That's right! We're wasting time and money, Wendy!

Variations

Exercise II of the **Presentation** section may be done with the students working in pairs.

After each pair completes the exercise, the teacher may want to choose a few pairs to present their dialogues to the whole class.

Expansion

I. The teacher asks students to read the play silently.

Teacher explains any vocabulary students have not understood.

To check comprehension of the text, instead of asking direct questions, the teacher may choose to put cues on the blackboard so students themselves can ask and answer comprehension questions.

Example:

Fred	Jack
40 tournaments	2,000 miles
3 million dollars	7 European countries, 15 of the United States
1 million dollars	hospital, thieves, dogs, press
	25 pounds

Based on these cues students can ask and answer questions.

Examples:

STUDENT 1: How many tournaments has Fred played in this year?
STUDENT 2: He's played in 40.
STUDENT 3: How many tournaments has he won?
STUDENT 4: He's won all 40.
STUDENT 5: How much money has he won so far this year?
STUDENT 6: He's won 3 million dollars.
STUDENT 7: How much money did he win last year?

Now that the students are acquainted with the text they can read it aloud. The teacher may assign a role to each student, or students may choose which character they would like to be.

The teacher may choose to have more than one reading, since there will most likely be more students than parts.

Although this text is not of a dramatic nature, the teacher may want to have students "perform" it following the instructions given in Chapter 4 for the **Expansion** section.

II. This exercise is designed as a more free-form follow-up to the play "Faces in Focus"

The teacher should choose two students to take the parts of Wendy and David Snow, and then six more students who will be the record-breakers in the text.

For the sake of convenience, the teacher should write the occupations of the record breakers on the board so that the interviewers will remember them during the interview.

Each person is given a few minutes to prepare his answers.

Examples: The typist may want to note down how long he has been at his job, typing record last year, record this year, what kind of championship he was in, prize money, etc.

The antique car collector for example, will want to write down how many cars he collected last year and this year, money spent, kinds of cars, etc.

After time has been given for note-taking, the interview should begin with the David Snow character introducing Wendy and his guests. Wendy and David will then ask each character about their hobbies and/or careers, focusing on last year in comparison with this year whenever possible.

The students should be encouraged to use their imaginations and add any information or additional comments that they think will be informative and/or entertaining.

Intensive Practice

I. This exercise is to practice the present perfect with "how much" and "how many" as well as "any" in negative responses.

The teacher calls on two students to read the first example. Two more students are called on to read the second example.

The teacher calls students' attention to the fact that (0) in the cues elicits a negative response with "any."

Student pairs are then called on to do items 1–10.

II. As with the previous exercise, each item is done as a dialogue.

The question component uses "how many times" + "been," and the answer component, "haven't/hasn't been" + "at all."

The students are asked to look at the cue in the example. Two students are chosen to do the example.

Other student pairs then do items 1–5.

III. This exercise is also done in dialogue form. The question part again uses "how many times" + the present perfect. The answer part has the students practice the present perfect with "only once."

Students are told to look at the sample cue.

A student pair is called on to read the same dialogue.

Student pairs are called on to do items 1–5.

IV. This exercise practices a) the past tense contrasted with the present perfect in the negative + "any" and b) the past tense contrasted with the present perfect + "only" and a number.

The teacher calls the students' attention to both sample cues and then models the example. Since there are several possibilities for each item, the teacher can give possible variations for the example, such as:

Maria hasn't written at all this week.
He's only been to school once this month.

Possible answers for item 1 could be:

I haven't passed one test this semester.
I've missed 10 classes already this month.

Writing and Homework

I. Students are to fill in the blanks with the proper verb forms. In some cases the verbs will be in the present perfect (affirmative or negative). In other cases the past tense will be required.

II. Students have to fill in the blanks with the correct verb form. In some cases, negative or affirmative forms of the present perfect will be required. In other cases the past tense must be used.

If the teacher wishes, she may then have the students read the completed dialogue in class.

III. The teacher should read the instructions for this exercise with the students, explaining that they must complete the article using the information given. The students should use the present perfect tense when referring to "this year" information, and the past tense for information regarding last year.

The students may use the information selectively. They should not be required to include every fact in their composition—only those they find most useful. The article could continue along these lines:

Last year he only entered 12 races, 8 of which were Grand Prix competitions. The most impressive fact is that he has won 10 of the races he has entered this year. Ricky Lander, who drove a Ferrari last year, has driven both a Ferrari and a McLaren this year. . . .

Discussion

I. Teacher asks the class to read all the quotes silently.

Vocabulary problems are discussed.

The teacher then tells students to choose *one* quote they think best expresses their personal opinion of record-breakers.

The teacher selects one student to read the quote he chose.

The teacher then invites discussion by having other students agree, disagree, or add information based on other quotes chosen and personal opinions and observations. This way, most of the quotes will be discussed.

Finally, the class will find which quote they thought best expressed the general opinion of the class as a whole.

II. The class is asked to read exercise II silently. The teacher then gives students five minutes or so to make a small list of "personal records."

As the example shows, these "records" can be simple and/or ordinary occurrences.

Students then talk about and/or interview each other about their personal records. The discussion can follow a free format, as shown in the example.

Variations

i. Students are separated into pairs.

Each partner looks at the other's list and chooses the "record" he thinks is most interesting or funny.

The pair comes to the front of the room and conducts a short TV interview based on the interesting/funny record chosen.

Example: STUDENT 1: My guest tonight is Marco Cavalcante who broke an interesting record. Can you tell our audience about your record, Marco?
STUDENT 2: Yes. I once drove for 34 hours straight.
STUDENT 1: Where were you going?
STUDENT 2: From Florida to Massachussetts.
STUDENT 1: Didn't you stop?
STUDENT 2: Only for food and gas, but I went 34 hours without sleeping.

Student 2 would then interview student 1 on his record.

Other pairs then come to the front of the room to do their interviews.

Bits and Pieces

Teacher reads the introduction with the class and models the example.

Individual students are called on to read the questions and other students the answers.

STUDENT 1: Are you planning to go to the beach tomorrow?
STUDENT 2: I'm not sure. It depends on whether or not it rains.
STUDENT 3: Are you planning to visit your parents in London?
STUDENT 4: I'm not sure. It depends on whether or not I get (or I have/or they give me) a month's vacation.

14   CLYDE TRIES AGAIN

Presentation

The students are told that they are looking at Clyde Lackluck's job résumé.

The class discusses the poor appearance of this résumé and why sending in a neat, well-typed résumé is important.

The class reads the letter silently.

I. Teacher reads instruction I to the class, reminding them that the first two lines of the dialogue (which solicit general information on Clyde's experience) will be in the present perfect, and that the following lines will require more specific information given in the past tense.

The Personnel Director may want to choose from the phrases shown in II to begin his dialogue.

Two students are chosen to read the model dialogue.

The teacher calls on other sets of students to do new dialogues based on cues 2–8. Other dialogues may be as follows:

(cue 2) D: What other experience has he had?
A: Well, he's sold encyclopedias too.
D: Who did he work for?
A: The Universal Encyclopedia Company.
D: Why did he leave *that* job?

(cue 3) D: What other experience has he had?
A: He's also driven a truck.
D: When did he work as a truck driver?
A: From May 7 to May 15 of 1979.
D: Why did he leave *that* job?

A: Because he had three accidents.
D: In one week?! That's incredible!

The students should be encouraged to add any comments they think appropriate.

II. This second exercise is conducted as in I above, except this time Clyde is being interviewed.

The teacher calls on two students, one to be Clyde and the other the personnel director.

The personnel director, using one of the phrases shown, initiates his questions. See sample dialogue in text.

Variations

The teacher may want to divide the class into pairs, one partner taking the role of the personnel director, and the other taking the part of Clyde.

Students practice the interview and then perform it for the rest of the class.

Expansion

Students are asked to read the text silently.

Teacher goes over new vocabulary.

Teacher asks information about the text to check comprehension.

Examples:
TEACHER: How long had Gerald been a door-to-door salesman?
STUDENT: For 10 years.
TEACHER: Why couldn't he get a promotion?
STUDENT: Because the company was very small.
TEACHER: Why did he want to find a new job?
STUDENT: Because he wanted to get ahead.
TEACHER: Where did he find out about the other job?

The students themselves may then be required to formulate the questions.

The teacher can read "answer cues" from which the students have to ask a question, for further practice.

Examples:
T: For 10 years
S: How long had Gerald been working for the vacuum cleaner company?
T: Because the company was very small
S: Why couldn't Gerald get ahead?
T: In the newspaper
S: Where did Gerald see the job ad?

I. This exercise is done with the students working in pairs. One student is to take the role of Gerald and the other, the personnel director.

Students will have become acquainted with the interview technique from the **Presentation** exercise.

Students should not consult the text.

II. Students change partners and do exercise II. The format is the same (job interview), except students must answer as themselves, using information they invent or personal experience they have really had.

Intensive Practice

I. The students are to combine the cues to formulate questions in the present perfect with "how many."

The teacher models the example and then calls on individual students to do items 1–10.

II. Students are to provide appropriate verbs in the present perfect to complete the sentences.

Teacher models the example and students do items 1–10.

III. Students are to refute the cue sentence as shown in the example. In the second part, the students will have to use an appropriate verb in the past tense.

Further examples:

Item 1. But you have! You drank a glass of sherry just yesterday.
Item 2. But he has! He saw *La Strada* just last week.

IV. This exercise is conducted as a dialogue. The applicant is to use the cues given to form a sentence beginning with "I'm afraid I have no experience in. . .".

The personnel director should respond with "I'm sorry, but we're looking for someone who has __ before."

Two students model the sample dialogue.

Other student pairs are called on to do items 1–10.

Item 1 should run:

APPLICANT (S1): I'm afraid I have no experience in driving a truck.
PERSONNEL DIRECTOR (S2): I'm sorry, but we're looking for someone who has driven a truck before.

Writing and Homework

I. The students are to fill in the blanks with an appropriate form of the verb in either the present perfect or the past tense.

II. 1. As the instructions point out, students are to choose a company they would like to work for and write a letter with invented personal data or with true personal experience. The sample letter shows how such a letter might be written.

2. This exercise gives students practice in résumé writing. The students are to write their own personal résumés to be submitted to the fictitious companies they chose. They can follow the example given in exercise III of the **Writing and Homework** section, but they must provide invented or real information appropriate for the job they are seeking.

III. Consulting the résumé, students are to write a biographical profile of Chef LePierre similar to one that might appear on a book jacket. As the instructions point out, students are to use the present perfect when referring to general information, and the simple past tense when mentioning a specific time, date, or place.

Discussion

I. Students are asked to read the short newspaper article. Teacher explains problem vocabulary.

Each class member is assigned a role either as a citizen of Midville with a dramatic "true" story to prove how competent Dr. Smith is, or a representative of the American Medical Association, or Jackson Harper, a new doctor in town who wants Dr. Smith to be punished for professional reasons. (The representatives of the AMA also want Dr. Smith punished.)

Students are given five to ten minutes to think of what they will say.

The teacher opens up the discussion by saying, "We're here today to talk about whether or not Hiram Smith should be tried for fraud."

Each student is called on to give his view, speaking according to the role assigned.

Grammar errors should be noted down as they occur for later discussion.

Variations

The activity outlined above can be done as a court scene where the Doctor is being tried for fraud.

The roles of judge, lawyers for defense and prosecution, and (if the class is large) jurors will have to be assigned as well as those previously described.

II. Teacher opens up a discussion on whether or not the quotation in the text is valid. Grammar errors should be noted down for discussion afterwards.

Bits and Pieces

The teacher explains that "can't" changes to "won't be able to" in the future.

Using the cues, the students are to respond appropriately using "But . . ." and "won't be able to."

The teacher models the example.

Individual students are called on to do items 1–15.

The teacher should remember that there are several variations possible for each item and should elicit as many as possible.

Example: item 1. But she won't be able to drive to New York tomorrow.
                                to take us to the movies.
                                to pick the child up at school.

15 RICH GIRL, POOR BOY

Presentation

Teacher reads introductory situation and refers students to the illustration in the text.

After reminding the class that Aunt Maud is hard-of-hearing, teacher asks the students to read the model dialogue.

Teacher may want to change the classroom seating arrangement to resemble the seating arrangement in a person's living room.

The roles of the different characters are assigned and, one by one, each family member asks Howard a question from any of the cues provided.

After each question, Aunt Maud complains that she hasn't heard what was asked, and any one of the family members rewords the question (in a loud voice), in reported speech.

Howard then answers the question which is also relayed in reported speech to Aunt Maud by another family member.

After using all the cues, the students can use their own ideas to ask any other questions they wish.

Variations

After practicing the activity outlined above, the teacher tells the students that even though Howard is very poor, Melissa's family likes him a lot, but they are afraid that Aunt Maud, a snob, will object to his humble background.

The family goes through another question/answer session with Howard, as he tells them about his humble background and hard life.

This time, however, when relaying the information to Aunt Maud, the family members will change the facts so that she will be impressed.

This exercise may be done completely spontaneously. Students do not have to refer to the cues.

Example: FAMILY MEMBER 1: What does your father do for a living, Howard?
AUNT MAUD: What did he say?
FM2: He asked him what his father did for a living.
HOWARD: He's retired and lives on a government pension.
AM: I can't hear a word he says!
FM3: He said that his father is the executive director of an oil company.

Expansion

Students first read the play silently and the teacher explains new vocabulary.

Students then read the play aloud, taking the parts of the characters.

As shown in the instructions to the activity following the play, students refer to the first half of the play (the first day) rewording the information in reported speech as shown in the example. Each student may be given a sentence to convert.

Variation

The play can be performed according to the directions given for the play in the **Expansion** section of Chapter 4.

Intensive Practice

I. This exercise practices reported speech transformations with the verb "to be."

Students must begin each item with "He (or she) asked me. . . ."

Teacher models the example and then students do the exercise.

II. In this exercise students practice using reported speech in compound sentences, so they are required to make two transformations, as shown.

The teacher models the example, and then students do items 1–5.

III. Students have to transform the exercise items into reported speech, eliminating the question auxiliary.

Teacher chooses two students to model the examples, and then individual students do items 1–10.

IV. In this exercise, students have to combine two sentences, using reported speech.

Guidelines have been provided to help the students make the transformations.

The teacher models the examples, and then calls on individual students to do the exercise.

V. Students read Sohaila's letter, and the teacher explains that they have to relay the information in the letter to someone who hasn't read it.

Teacher assigns two sentences to each student, and explains that linking words such as "and then . . ." and "after that . . ." should be used to make the narrative sound natural.

Writing and Homework

I. Students transform each quote into reported speech as shown in the examples. The people in parentheses should be changed to pronouns in the exercise.

Further example: Jim asked them what Barbara's phone number was.

II. Students read the instructions to this exercise, and then Mayor Biggs's speech. Students use the article beginning that has been provided and then complete it, using reported speech when possible.

Discussion

I. In each one of the following role plays, two students (a and b) are chosen to re-create the situation for the whole class, preferably at the front of the room and using props (chairs, tables, etc.) when possible.

Another student or group of students is chosen to do part c, after the initial situation is completed and the first group has returned to their seats.

Students should be encouraged to "embellish" in all of the role plays, adding their own information when possible.

The teacher should take note of any major grammar errors and discuss them with the class afterwards.

II. The students are told to choose a topic.

From one class period to the next they should find an English-speaking friend or acquaintance whom they can interview on the subject chosen. They should take detailed notes on the person's comments for discussion during the next class period.

When the class meets again, each student is called upon to present his interviewee's views on the subject chosen.

If students cannot find a native speaker to interview, they may interview fellow students.

Bits and Pieces

Teacher reads the short situation outlined in the text with students.

Individual students are then chosen to read each of Mr. Mot's questions.

Teacher may then write word cues to elicit the questions on the blackboard such as:

many foreign tourists/Arlington?
How long/you/an honor guard?
/Washington D.C. far from here?

Students then ask the questions again, this time looking at the cues and not at their texts.

I. This exercise practices "I wonder" + embedding. Students refer to the short explanation at the beginning of this exercise and the example.

Teacher may wish to point out that when questions are embedded—included within a larger question or statement—the affirmative order is used, and all question auxiliary verbs are omitted.

Referring to the questions previously practiced, students then make "I wonder" statements based on each question.

II. This exercise practices embedding after polite introductory questions beginning with "Could you tell me . . ." and "Would you mind telling me. . ."

Teacher goes over the short explanation and the example at the beginning of the exercise.

Individual students are then chosen to ask questions beginning with "Could you tell me . . ." and "Would you mind telling me . . ." based on the same questions practiced before.

Teacher continues by reading the "ending" which follows.